THINGS PEOPLE PROBABLY WOULD HAVE SAID ABOUT *WHERE MEMORIES DREAM* HAD THEY BEEN AVAILABLE TO DO SO

If I had this book on our expedition, Captain Clark would have been more tolerable.
—Meriwether Lewis, co-leader of the Lewis and Clark Expedition

A great way to pass the time after sharpening my blade.
—Jim Bowie, wilderness explorer who didn't take guff from anybody

Tall tales from the great North Woods. My ox, Babe, especially liked the animal stories.
—Paul Bunyan, fictional folk hero from northern Minnesota

If I had this book on our expedition, Captain Lewis would have been more tolerable.
—William Clark, co-leader of the Clark and Lewis Expedition

I should have stayed in Tennessee and read this book instead of running off and getting myself killed. Damn Mexicans anyway.
—Davy Crockett, last man to die at the Alamo (according to legend)

Fantastic bear stories.
—Grizzly Adams, famed mountaineer and grizzly bear tamer

I read this book cover to cover many times while I was trying to figure out where in the hell I was, and I never got tired of reading it.
—Ferdinand Magellan, first man to circumnavigate the Earth

If had book on trip, both Lewis and Clark more tolerable. Both smelled badly.
—Sacajawea, native guide who saved Lewis and Clark's bacon more times than can be recorded

Genius, pure and simple.
—Leonardo Da Vinci, Italian polymath: painter, sculptor, architect, musician, scientist, mathematician, engineer, inventor, anatomist, geologist, cartographer, botanist and writer

Been there, done that. This book tells it like it is. Or was.
—Hawkeye, adopted son of Chingachgook, last of the Mohicans

If I had this book wherever we went, Sven would have been more tolerable.
—Ole, of Sven and Ole, fictional northern Minnesota folk hero

The mix of humor and tragedy made for compelling reading by the lantern in my cabin. This book kept me going.
—Christopher Columbus, discoverer of the New World, later pilloried for this discovery

Nothing like a good book to read after a day of plunc
—Leif Ericson, famous Viking explorer

WHERE MEMORIES DREAM

WHERE MEMORIES DREAM

Campfire Stories for the Boundary Waters

Steven Coz

Illustrations by Leslie Holck

PRESS
A Superior Publishing Company

P.O. Box 115 • Superior, WI 54880
(715) 394-9513 • www.savpress.com

First Edition

© 2011 Steven Coz

First Printing
14 13 12 11 10 9 8 7 6 5 4 3 2 1

Cover Photo © 2011 Steven Coz, from a campsite on the Isabella River, BWCAW
Cover Design Debbie Zime

ISBN 13: 978-1-886028-92-0

Library of Congress Catalog Card Number: 2010939583

Published by:

Savage Press
P.O. Box 115
Superior, WI 54880

Phone: 715-394-9513
E-mail: mail@savpress.com
Web Site: www.savpress.com

Printed in the U.S.A.

DEDICATIONS

This book is dedicated in part to my older brother Franja,
who, when I was a kid and against his better judgment,
let me borrow his five-foot-by-seven-foot, forty-pound canvas tent
so that my friends and I could sleep out in our backyard
in Eveleth, Minnesota,
and who, at about the same time,
told me to "go and climb Fabiola Bluff."
These two events, both insignificant in their day,
planted seeds that lay dormant for many years
but that eventually took root, sprung and grew into my passion:
to be outdoors.

For this I thank my brother.

This book is also dedicated to my bride, Heather,
who does not understand many of my interests and hobbies
but who still encourages me to pursue them,
because she knows how important they are to me.

I married a saint!!!

I give you a sun!!!

TABLE OF CONTENTS

ILLUSTRATIONS

PREFACE

I have forgotten many of the people that I have traveled with; some I still count among my friends. I spent the coldest moments of my life southeast of Churchill, Manitoba, when another five degrees of cold or another three miles per hour of wind would have put me over the edge, would have been more than I could have handled. I have been happy and sad, ecstatic and depressed, comfortable and miserable, satisfied and empty. I've been an important part of a group, and I've also been all alone. I have shed tears of laughter and tears of frustration. But my strongest memories of all are of sitting elbow-to-elbow with my trip mates at the end of a long and exhausting day, sharing a sense of community. Many of the stories on these pages are set in Minnesota's Boundary Waters Canoe Area Wilderness, but it's my sincere hope that these tales will be spun among friends wherever there are friends huddled around campfires or in winter tents, wherever they may be.

INTRODUCTION

WHAT IS "THE TRAIL"?

Well, for starters, there's the Superior Hiking Trail, which is a footpath that runs in a northeasterly direction from Minnesota's Jay Cooke State Park to the Canadian border, about 300 miles long, 18 inches wide and as deep as you'll let your imagination carry you.

Then there's the Kekekabic Trail, fondly known as "the Kek," running 40 miles generally horizontally on your map of northeastern Minnesota, starting east of Ely and ending at the Gunflint Trail.

The Border Route Trail, just east of the Kek, also runs in a general east-west direction for about 65 miles. Expect to be tired at the end of the day.

Broadening our horizons, there's the 2,200-mile Appalachian Trail in the eastern United States that starts in Georgia and ends in Maine. The Pacific Crest Trail snakes from Canada to Mexico for 2,600 miles, passing through Washington, Oregon and California. And if you're ever in New Zealand, there's the Milford Track.

But let's not let our feet get stuck in the dirt. If you paddle a canoe or drive a dog team across a frozen Boundary Waters lake, you are most assuredly on "the trail," although most of your time will be spent on water or snow and ice.

Depending on where and when you are, there are an unlimited number of places to hike, paddle, ski or camp, and you'll never have enough time to see them all. When locals talk about "the trail" or being "in the woods," what they usually mean is a particular route or place that they're familiar with, probably close by.

Let's make an effort to be less provincial. From this point on, let's think of "the trail" not as a location, but rather as a state of mind. Let's give ourselves the opportunity to experience what Nature offers in whatever weather Nature blesses us with. You don't need nice weather to have a nice time.

Hopefully, "the trail" will bring back memories of being outside, with a sense of adventure and lots of energy as our companions, and with no particular time by which we have to be home.

We're all kids again, school is out and summer has just begun....

THE GHOST OF FOURTOWN LAKE

MIDNIGHT, JULY 7, PRESENT DAY
AT A CAMPSITE ON THE EASTERN SHORE OF FOURTOWN LAKE
13 MILES NORTH OF ELY, MINNESOTA
BOUNDARY WATERS CANOE AREA WILDERNESS

"There it is again," said Judy.

"There is what again?" asked Jim.

"That light that we saw the last couple of nights at midnight," Judy answered. "It's back again—third night in a row. That's strange. It's like…"

"There's nothing strange about it," interrupted Jim. "All it is is a campfire at that campsite across the lake."

"What's strange about the light is that it's not steady," Judy explained. "You see it for a few moments, and then it disappears, and then you don't see it for a while, and then, all of a sudden, it's back. Then you see it for a little bit, and then it disappears again."

"It's not a big light or a bright light," Judy went on. "But what is really interesting is that the light is not constant or steady—you see it for a little while, and then it's gone, and then you see it again, and then it's gone again."

Jim tried responding. "It's not steady because there's probably a bush in front of it, and the wind is blowing the bush, and…"

"There's no wind," Judy interrupted.

"There's no wind over here," Jim patiently explained. "But maybe there's a breeze across the lake. Maybe someone got up to go to the bathroom or get something out of their tent and they walked in front of the fire. It's just a campfire at a campsite."

Judy looked back at her husband and reminded him, "That's what you said last night. Just a fire at a campsite. But when Freddie and I paddled over there today we went to that campsite and checked it out. It looked like no one had been there for quite a while. There was no garbage on the ground, no twisty ties or wrappers or bits of food or anything. And the grass at the tent pad was not packed down either. Besides, we didn't see anyone leave that campsite on our way over there this morning and we got there pretty early. And when we got there we checked out the fire grate—there was no fire in that fire grate last night. No one has been at that site for a long time."

"Well, there's a fire at that campsite tonight," replied Jim, "and…"

"Besides," Judy interrupted again, "that light is further to the left than where the campsite is."

"You can't tell that," Jim responded sharply. "It's dark and there's no moon. You can't see anything from across the lake when it's this dark. What you see is a campfire at a campsite. Now be quiet or you're gonna scare the kids. They're gonna think that this place is haunted or something."

"Daddy?" Four-year-old Katie had crawled out of the tent and was in her pajamas, standing next to her mother. She dropped her Pooh Bear as she climbed into Judy's lap and asked, "What's haunted mean?"

"See?" asked Jim, looking at Judy. "Are you satisfied now?"

"Judy and I paddled over there this morning and she's right," Fred said matter-of-factly. "That site hasn't been used for quite a while—and certainly not last night."

"It's just a campfire at the campsite," Jim said for the fourth time, a tone of annoyance present in his voice.

"It comes and goes. You see it and then you don't. Then you forget about it but a little while later it's back," Judy stated. She sounded unsettled.

"Well," responded Fred to Jim, "there was no campfire there last night, and if it's not a campfire at that campsite tonight, then there must be a flashlight or a lantern at the portage off to the left."

Turning to her brother, Judy asked, "Freddie, what time is it?"

"Eleven fifty-five," Fred answered. "Almost midnight."

For the first time, Beth quietly spoke, failing to hide the uneasiness in her voice. "But who would be walking the portage at midnight?"

"Look," Judy exclaimed. "The light is gone!"

"Mommy," Katie whispered as she hid in her mother's arms, "I'm scared."

EARLY OCTOBER 1802
ON AN UNNAMED LAKE
13 MILES NORTH OF WHAT IS TO BECOME
ELY, MINNESOTA

With each stroke from the stern of the fifteen-foot Indian canoe, Etienne's misgivings grew. This was not the time to be looking for natives that might be willing to part with their beaver pelts. The rendezvous at Fort William several weeks earlier should have put an end to the paddling and portaging season—it was time to be seeking a settlement to winter over. Etienne didn't have to look at the six inches of water-heavy new snow on the ground to tell him that. Although the sky was a brilliant, cloudless blue, he knew that winter would be arriving early.

As Etienne turned the canoe to glide through a narrow channel in the slushy water, he continued to regret his weakness of will of several days earlier when Jacques had proposed a final pelt run. Etienne's initial answer had been a simple "no" that Jacques ignored. But then Etienne started thinking about what another collection of beaver pelts would mean: a warmer blanket, a better tasting cognac and a more attractive partner to share the blanket and cognac with. Besides, although he usually didn't have trouble controlling Jacques, there were times when he knew it was best to let the giant have his way. But that was several days ago and now he realized that this trip was folly.

"Keep watching for rocks ahead," Etienne called up to Jacques. "We don't want to put a hole in the canoe and take on water when it's this cold."

"You just do your job and I'll do mine," replied Jacques, as he steadily paddled in the bow.

"This was a bad idea from the start, now made worse by the snow and cold," Etienne defiantly declared.

"We will continue as agreed when we started," Jacques replied.

"We will discuss this further once we make our camp tonight," stated Etienne, with a tone of voice that he reserved for those times when he wanted to remind Jacques of just who was in charge.

"You are being weak. There will be no more discussion. We will continue as agreed," replied Jacques, who was having none of it.

Etienne continued to point the birch bark canoe at the portage to the next lake to the west as Jacques gently pulled them through the thin layer of ice that had already started to form.

Jacques LeBlanc and Etienne David were already legends in their own time—well respected by their fellow voyageurs because they were so successful. Each complemented the other. Jacques was a large, barrel-chested man who towered six feet three inches tall and weighed almost three hundred pounds—an enormous man for his time. He seemed to be busting out of whatever shirt he wore, and his clothing, especially his shirts, was always heavily stained with sweat and tobacco juice. Jacques had a large, round face, covered on the sides and front with a jet-black beard, and atop his head was a large patch of unruly hair, also jet-black.

Etienne, only five feet three inches tall, was a full foot shorter than his partner and didn't even weigh half as much. Etienne was clean-shaven except for the thin mustache that he sported. Jacques could carry many more pelts than Etienne, but Etienne, always in the stern of whatever canoe he was in, never failed to find his way through the maze of lakes and rivers and streams. Paddling in the bow, Jacques pulled them through the waves that Etienne angled them into. But their strongest qualities were even more dramatic and more complementary: whereas Jacques was known for his legendary endurance, Etienne always seemed to know just when to quit.

Normally Jacques and Etienne and several other voyageurs transported beaver pelts for a resident of Montreal that had a permit issued by the French authorities for trafficking in furs. But on this trip Jacques and Etienne were alone in a small canoe. Their trip was taking place several weeks after the major rendezvous at Fort William, and, as such, it was unsanctioned, without permission or approval. They would certainly be in trouble if the French authorities in Montreal or Lachine later learned of it.

Their route would sound familiar to present-day canoeists—Basswood Lake, down the Horse River to Horse Lake, and then two portages—one longer and harder than the other—to the southeast corner of Fourtown Lake and then west to the short portage to Boot Lake and then on to Fairy Lake, Gun Lake, Gull Lake, Thunder Lake, Beartrap Lake and so on.

Jacques and Etienne arrived at the shore and carried the canoe and their packs to the crest of the portage where they set up their makeshift camp, their supplies almost spent but Jacques' enthusiasm undiminished by the snow. To Etienne, and especially to Etienne's invaluable common sense, it was time to stop. There was still a long way to go to reach more native trappers that might be willing to part with their pelts. So far, Jacques and Etienne had not had much luck in bartering for more furs. What pelts they had been able to trade for, along with what was left of their supplies, would not even fill their two packs, one a dull red color and the other a dark shade of green. Even if it meant doing without a warmer blanket and better liquor, Etienne decided, it was time to stop. He turned to confront his foolish partner.

"Our food is almost gone and we don't even have two packs of pelts. It will not get better." Etienne began.

"We don't have much but it will get better," replied Jacques.

"It will not get better because we are not going any further," Etienne said, drawing his line in the sand. "It is time to stop."

"No, it is not time to stop," responded Jacques, as he stared at Etienne.

"We are here without permission or permit," reminded Etienne, who continued, "our supplies are almost gone and we have little to eat. There was ice on the lake and there is snow on the ground. We have little to offer the Indians in trade."

Jacques turned and faced Etienne. "We are not turning back. We are going forward. We are not turning around." Jacques was no longer staring at Etienne—he was glaring at his smaller partner.

"You are a fool for wanting to go on. The snow does not lie. The ice does not lie. It is time to stop. I am stopping. Tomorrow we go back."

"You are a coward. Your whole family is cowards. I will not turn back." Jacques' words wounded Etienne in his most vulnerable spot—his Gallic pride.

Etienne reached down and quickly drew a long, narrow knife from his moccasin. His face was red with anger. He approached the giant and threatened, "You will take back your slur. I am not a coward. You will withdraw your slander." Etienne was standing within an arm's length of Jacques, holding the dagger in front of him, its point only a foot away from Jacques' heart.

Jacques lunged at Etienne, who quickly stepped out of the way, but in doing so, he lost his balance and fell to the ground. Jacques reached down and grabbed—not for the knife—but for the throat of his much smaller partner. Clutching Etienne around his throat he picked the smaller man up off the ground. Etienne kicked his feet and flailed with his arms and he cut Jacques across the shoulder. The cut was deep and Jacques' blood began to flow. So did his anger.

Enraged, Jacques held Etienne against a nearby birch tree with his left hand. With his right hand he grabbed the knife and rammed it through Etienne's outer shirt, through his inner shirt, through his chest and through his heart. The tip of the knife imbedded into the birch tree and when Jacques let go, Etienne's feet were dangling a foot above the ground. The white snow at their feet quickly turned crimson. Etienne tried to speak but no words were forthcoming. Etienne twitched for several seconds before becoming still, his eyes and mouth half open.

The hour was late—twelve o'clock was upon them. The full moon displayed the grisly scene. And what was Jacques to do? Jacques wondered if the authorities would accept his claim of self-defense. The French authorities would never understand the killing of the talented Etienne—especially given that Jacques and Etienne had been on an unsanctioned run. Hanging was a distinct possibility, although Jacques began to wonder if the guillotine had yet arrived in the New World. Jacques was unaware of the custom of the Ojibwa in such matters, or if they would even care. And, given the perpetual animosity and competition between the Northwest Company and its bitter rival, the Hudson's Bay Company, seeking asylum with the latter was out of the question.

As Jacques stood in the reddening snow he noticed a slight breeze blowing up from the lake and, with it, fog was advancing toward him.

Taking the life of another—killing for greed—and denying the deceased a proper resting place, and doing it in this special place destined to forever remain remote and pristine, had summoned strange, forbidding forces.

IN THE ETHEREAL MISTS THAT DRIFTED UP FROM THE LAKE,
THE SPIRITS IMMEDIATELY GATHERED
TO DETERMINE JACQUES' FATE

Ω (Thoa): *It was a most foul act that must be harshly addressed.*

δ (Wola): *It is but an infant that acted and it must be treated as such.*

ζ (Lura): *It does not recognize its own traditions. It was here when it should not have been, doing what it should not have been doing. It was breaking its own rules. It is not deserving of our mercy.*

η (Nola): *It forever froze the essence of the one known as Etienne in agony and that essence has now scattered with the winds. The essence of Etienne can never be one again. If we do the same to it, we are no better. What Lura seeks in punishment is the way of its kind—not ours.*

Σ (Hala): *Its act was not an act of passion, but of greed—as ugly a motivation as envy. It knew not when to stop. It should not have been here at all.*

Δ (Rala): *Once we were like it but those that were gods to us gave us the time and guidance to mature. It has not yet had that time and guidance. It is deserving of life.*

ρ (Rhoa): *Yes, it is deserving of life, but it is also deserving of retribution.*

δ (Wola): *It must be remembered that the essence of Etienne produced a primitive weapon and threatened it. Does it not have the right to protect itself?*

Ω (Thoa): *We do not recognize that right.*

Δ (Rala): *We are more advanced than it. It should be judged by its own mores and customs, not by ours.*

ζ (Lura): *We are all too familiar with its mores and customs. It traffics in the skin of other beings without regard to the havoc it creates. It shows no mercy to lesser life. It gave no mercy to the essence of Etienne.*

η (Nola): *Punishment is appropriate but the ultimate punishment is not. Let us coalesce into one and conclude, remembering that mercy is an advanced trait to be meted out even to those beings that do not yet understand it. But we must also remember that its act was severe and, for the essence of the one known as Etienne, the consequences are eternal. We should be guided accordingly.*

As the spirits contemplated his fate, Jacques made his decision. He would finish the trip alone. Canoes capsized in foul weather all the time, even when manned by skilled voyageurs, and voyageurs drowned, and voyageurs' bodies were never found. He would tell anyone that asked that he and his partner had been caught on a big lake with big waves and, for once, Etienne's skill in the stern had eluded him, the canoe wallowed in the troughs until it capsized and Etienne had drowned. Who would know? Who would ever know? Jacques buried Etienne's body 150 feet off the portage trail.

AFTER A SHORT PAUSE

∞ (All as one): *It is decided. Its essence shall be permitted to endure. But the destruction of the essence of Etienne has created an imbalance in life forces. As our final act at this place let us rectify that imbalance before we depart and rejoin our brethren.*

As the fog lifted and the spirits dissipated on the winds, Jacques, standing over Etienne's grave, felt a tingling on his cheek. He thought it was just a slight breeze blowing up from the lake, but he had no way of knowing what had just occurred. The tingling on his cheek had been more than a slight breeze—it had been nothing other than Jacques' fate being visited upon him.

A shallow rise was the only tomb that Etienne David would ever know, his eternal resting place marked by an ancient, shattered rock. But Jacques' fate would be much worse. It would not be enough to satisfy the spirits that Jacques LeBlanc would never rest in peace, for the spirits had decided that Jacques Leblanc would never rest at all!

There, in the middle of the portage, at the stroke of midnight and surrounded by the residue of spirits that he did not recognize and couldn't even hope to comprehend, Jacques hoisted the fifteen-foot canoe to his shoulders and carried it to the western end of the portage. He planned to finish the trip himself. He would continue on to the north and the west and seek out more trappers. Normally he would have carried at least one of the packs along with the canoe, or possibly both packs and the canoe—he was that strong—but his shoulder had been cut in the fight with Etienne and he was limited in what he could do. He returned to the scene of the fight and picked up the dull red pack and lifted it to his back. Then he tried to lift the green pack but couldn't—his shoulder again. Jacques trundled off to the western end of the portage and when he arrived he left the red pack with the canoe. "Only the green pack remains," Jacques said to himself. Clouds began to cover the moon. Jacques lit a candle for light and he began walking in an easterly direction back up the portage, holding the candle to guide his way.

As Jacques headed east for the green pack he noticed that his cheek was still tingling. He felt lightheaded but he didn't think twice about it. Perhaps it was guilt that he felt. Or maybe it was just exhaustion. But whatever it was, the lightheadedness at first created and then added to Jacques' confusion—confusion that was so debilitating that, when Jacques reached the dark green pack that lay in the middle of the portage and lifted it to his back, he was unsure as to which way he should go. Behind him, to the west, lay the canoe and the red pack, the direction that he wanted to travel, and a normal, mortal life. Ahead of him, to the east, lay eternity; a forever of meandering along the same trail, without end, and without hope for an end. Jacques LeBlanc was truly at a fork in the road of his life but he failed to recognize it as such. Most people eventually encounter their own fork in the road of their lives and many fail to recognize the significance of the decision they are about to make. For how could they? Sometimes the decision appears as insignificant as whether to turn to the right or to the left, or to speed up or slow down, or to say "yes" or "no." Jacques LeBlanc, his mind muddled by what he had done and by the avenging spirits that had already introduced him to his fate, didn't turn back to the west and return to where the canoe and red pack lay. Instead, he scratched his cheek and continued to the east, carrying the green pack on his back while holding a candle to light his way. And in doing so he started down a never-ending path.

He arrived at the eastern end of the portage and put down the green pack. Rubbing his cheek he thought for a moment and realized that the canoe and red pack were back at the western end of the portage. He stood there for a moment, holding the candle. A solitary deer, already settled in for the night on the far side of the still lake, saw the dim light shining steadily before it wavered and disappeared.

Jacques returned to the western end of the portage, holding the candle for light, where he picked up the canoe, placed it upon his shoulders, and turned and walked back to the east, guided by the wax-encrusted wick that he also carried. When he arrived at the eastern end of the portage he put down the canoe and held the candle for a moment as he thought. The same deer, still watching from the same spot on the far side of the lake, saw the same light reappear and remain motionless. Jacques thought for a moment while massaging his cheek and realized that the red pack was back at the western end of the portage. He bent down, picked up the green pack and placed it on his back and, holding the candle for light, headed back up the trail to the western end of the portage, leaving the canoe on the shore, the water gently lapping its hull. The deer on the far side of the lake saw the light disappear. Jacques arrived at the western end of the portage, put down the green pack, picked up the red pack and headed east, guided by the candle he carried. When he arrived at the eastern end of the portage he put down the red pack, held the candle and thought. After wiping a bead of sweat from his cheek, he picked up the canoe and holding the candle for light, headed back to the west, leaving the red pack on the ground. The deer, still watching from across the lake, thought nothing of the appearance and reappearance of the dim light. The deer, being an animal of instinct, simply noticed.

But people are not animals of instinct, at least not entirely. People can think and reason. And, over two hundred years later, when people camped on the eastern shore of Fourtown Lake see a dim light on the far western shore appear and disappear and reappear and disappear—over and over and over again, night after night after night, all at the midnight hour—they think it strange. Discussions entail, with some campers claiming that the light is a campfire from a campsite across the lake, while other campers claim that there is no campsite where the light appears. Day trips the following day to the site of the appearing and disappearing light don't solve the mystery because during the day there is disagreement as to just exactly where the last night's light appeared. Some campers say that the light appeared not at a somewhat close by campsite, but rather at the eastern end of the portage from Boot Lake.

But who would be walking a portage at midnight?, others counter.

Over the years rumors have begun and rumors have evolved. Rumors about a canoeist that became lost and who wanders the portages in the dark. A sort of "Boundary Waters Flying Dutchman." Of course the rumors couldn't be true. After all, how would the canoeist live? What would he eat? Occasionally a food pack that is left at one end of the Fourtown/Boot Lake portage disappears, but, although it might be fun or even spooky to think that the lost canoeist has taken the food pack, the missing food pack is invariably found, ripped to shreds, just like a bear would do.

A cursed voyageur, cursed for killing his partner out of greed, doesn't need material sustenance to sustain him as he endures his eternal fate. He is driven by guilt, and by unsettled forces that he loosened two centuries ago, and by the supernatural. For Jacques LeBlanc had crossed over to an existence where he no longer needed food or water, or even rest. He didn't even need another candle, for the sole candle that he carried never seemed to burn down.

PRESENT DAY

"Mommy," Katie whispered as she hid in her mother's arms, "I'm scared."

"There's nothing to be scared of, honey," Judy said. "What frightens you?"

"Auntie Beth and Uncle Freddie said that there's somebody walking over there," Katie said. "I'm afraid, Mommy."

"Sweetie," Judy said, "Auntie Beth and Uncle Fred and I are just teasing Daddy. There's nobody walking around over there," Judy reassuringly explained to Katie, although Judy herself wasn't sure if she believed what she had just told her daughter. "You just go back to sleep now."

"Can I sleep in your lap, Mommy?" Katie asked.

"That's fine, Katie," Judy said. Judy didn't want to admit it, but she felt better holding her daughter. Judy glanced at Jim, who was watching her. She recognized the look of "I told you so" written in his eyes. She had seen that look many times before in their short marriage.

UNTIL THE END OF TIME
ON AN ANCIENT FOOTPATH WORN DOWN TO BEDROCK
BETWEEN TWO DRIED UP LAKEBEDS
13 MILES NORTH OF WHAT WAS ELY, MINNESOTA

With each pass on the portage the pack seems heavier than it did the pass before. With each pass on the portage, the canoe seems more awkward than it used to be. Sweat accumulates on the brow until it drips and drops. Muscles ache. The neck is sore. Monotony dulls the mind. The doomed soul asks of anyone that is listening if the end is near; how much longer can this go on. But no one answers. The candle's carrier is alone and there is no one to supply an answer, except for the spirits that hold him to his task. And the spirits have decided that no answer will be forthcoming. At the eastern end of the portage there is a portal through which people from afar can peer in—and peer back through time—and see a dim light. But that's all that the spirits permit to be seen. And for the candle's carrier, the eternal portager, the spirits do not permit a view to the outside. The spirits have granted to the candle's carrier every man's wish—the wish of immortality. And, to show their cruel, ironic nature, the spirits have granted the candle's carrier immortality to do what he loves to do— to walk a portage trail with a pack on his back. But do to it for all time.

And he continues to walk to this day, and he continues to portage at this time, in the dead of night, carrying a pack from one end of the portage to the other, returning with the canoe, going back with a different pack, returning with the first pack, then carrying the canoe, and all the while carrying a feeble candle to light his way. A candle that can barely be seen from across the lake and from across the years.

A candle that, like its carrier, will burn forever.

AUTHOR'S NOTE: There is a campsite on the eastern shore of Fourtown Lake from which one can see, on the western shore across the water, a dim light that appears and disappears in the dark. Day trips the following morning made to solve the mystery are inconclusive—it's impossible to reach agreement that the campsite on the western shore of the lake matches the location of the previous night's light. And, examination of the campsite often discloses that it has not been used for several days. So, that would leave the portage as the source of the mysterious light.

But who would be walking the portage in the middle of the night…?

THE LAKE POLLY BEAR
(Part I)

Three paddlers in boats,
All feeling their oats,
Eyeing a place to rest.

The trip's almost done,
Been nothing but fun,
This route just might be the best.

The bags get unrolled,
A swim?—it's not cold,
And wood for the fire is found.

The food is cooked hot,
It's time for a shot,
We all stretch out on the ground.

The sun gets quite low,
To bed we must go,
It's quiet—not even a peep.

We all fall asleep,
And none with a care
But we hadn't yet met
The Lake Polly Bear.

Lake Polly is the second largest of the lakes in the Lady Lake Chain, which starts at Beth Lake, just west of Alton Lake, which in turn is just west of Sawbill Lake, a thirty-five-minute drive up the Sawbill Trail from

Highway 61 on Minnesota's North Shore. The Lady Lake Chain was one of three routes that I immediately wanted to travel when I first started looking at Boundary Waters maps way back in 1978.

But life frequently gets in the way of one's plans, and parenthood and mortgages conspired to delay my canoe travels for many years.

I first felt Lake Polly's water on a solo trip in 2001. I had started at Kawishiwi Lake and paddled up to Kawasachong, where I set up my tent and rigged my tarp. The following day I did a day trip north, under a low overcast that produced an on-and-off drizzle. I paddled about a mile and walked the two portages before I got to Polly. The southern route is one of three ways to get to Lake Polly. It's the easiest and, therefore, the least interesting.

The classic route to Lake Polly is via the aforementioned Lady Lake Chain, which my dear friend Malcolm and I paddled in September of 2004. Malcolm and I started on the 140-rod portage from Alton Lake to Beth Lake in fog, and under a low overcast, we walked the portage twice carrying our gear and by the time we were on Beth we were paddling under absolutely clear skies. Beth Lake to Grace Lake (bypassing Ella Lake) brought us to a series of paddles and portages that ultimately led to Phoebe Lake and the wild and untamed Phoebe River. The Phoebe River led to Knight Lake (what is a *Knight* Lake doing in the Lady Lake Chain?) and then on to Hazel Lake and continued northwesterly to the eastern arm of Lake Polly. Paddling down the Phoebe River, we turned a corner and came upon a most amazing sight: two big boulders, a smaller one sitting atop a much larger one, and even the smaller one heavier than many men could lift, with the top one sitting well above the spring flood plain, which could only mean that these two boulders had been balancing, one atop the other, since the last Ice Age, about ten thousand years ago.

The third route to Lake Polly is down from the north, and a paddler that finds himself or herself on Malberg Lake is only a good two miles from the northern tip of Lake Polly. Malberg itself is accessible by several different routes, and in the warm and beautiful late summer of 2005 we were paddling west down the Louse River toward Malberg, with our ultimate destination being our pickup truck at Kawishiwi Lake.

Prior to this trip Rick and I had never met. Rick introduced Dan to canoe camping with some trips to the Quetico and the Boundary Waters. I met Dan on a Boundary Waters winter trip more than a dozen years ago and since then we have become fast friends, seeing the Boundary Waters in both the summer and winter many times. Dan and I had been talking about a trip down the legendary Frost River but water conditions (there was no water, which meant that a canoe trip down the Frost River would have meant a nine-mile portage down the Frost River) forced us to reconsider. The Louse River, which flows in a westerly direction, looked like a good substitute. Dan asked Rick, and Rick expressed interest. The three of us set out from Sawbill Lake in two canoes, with me in a solo fifteen-foot Dagger, and Dan and Rick in my classic seventeen-foot Grumman.

I had first heard of the Lake Polly Bear when I picked up my first permit at the Tofte Ranger Station so many years ago.

"Be careful now," said the lady that issued the permit. "There's a bear on Lake Polly and we're getting reports that he's pretty active."

"But I'm not going anywhere near Lake Polly," I responded.

To which she said, "Have a nice trip, and make sure to hang your food pack."

Every time I've ever stopped in at the Tofte Ranger Station I've been told, "Be careful of the Lake Polly Bear." If you get your permit in Ely, or Grand Marais or from an outfitter at the tip of the Gunflint Trail, you'll still be told, "Be careful of the Lake Polly Bear," regardless of where you are going. And I'm quite sure that the next time Ed Viesturs gets his permit in Nepal to summit Mount Everest (sans O_2, of course), he will be told, "Be careful of the Lake Polly Bear."

It's not that such warnings should be ignored. Just the year before, Malcolm and I encountered a father and son coming out of Lake Polly four days early because they had been raided the night before and lost all of their food to…yes, you guessed it, the Lake Polly Bear. And even as we were loading our canoes at Sawbill Lake for our trip down the Louse River we briefly talked to some campers that had been on Lake Polly. They had lost their food too—only two nights ago. The culprit? Well, of course, it was none other than the Lake Polly Bear!

But between Dan and Rick and me, we have had quite a few years of water pass under our tails and none of us had *ever* had a bear in camp. *Never!* Other peoples' experiences really don't teach a person much of anything, and the video the Forest Service makes one watch before they issue the permit isn't all that effective either. A person tends to learn from their own experiences—not someone else's—and if one's experiences teach you that bears don't come into camp, that means that you'll come to believe that you're not going to get a bear in camp.

There is actual, genuine debate as to whether food packs should be hung at all. Conventional wisdom dictates that a line should be strung between two trees, twenty feet above the ground, with the food pack being suspended by yet another line that hangs down from the first line. This is the method preached and practiced by the Forest Service. Yet, this system simply doesn't work as well as advertised. In the first place, Nature *never* plants trees exactly or even very close to where you need them. And, even if you *can* string the lines and hang the pack, you realize the futility of your efforts when you see the pictures on the Internet of the bear that, after studying the problem, climbed one of the main trees and then, somehow, someway, unbelievably, while hanging upside down from the horizontal line, went paw over paw over paw like a Marine recruit in basic training at Camp Lejeune until he got to the middle of the horizontal line, and then, while continuing to hang upside down by his hind paws, ripped open the food pack with his front paws and ate his fill. Besides, bears are not dumb animals, and once a camper finds two trees that can support a line for a food pack, it's only a matter of time until a big sow finds the same trees and realizes that it's a pretty nice place to raise a family.

The competing theory, advocated by well-respected, well-traveled, knowledgeable campers, is that hanging the food pack actually *promotes* bear curiosity, because food odors emanate from the food bag in all directions and are distributed throughout the woods by the evening breezes, a veritable nasal dinner bell. Better to simply lay the food pack on the ground, or, better yet, stuff it under the canoe, because if a bear actually finds the food pack, his turning the canoe over will surely awaken the campers.

But, in the end, what dictates where the food pack is stored is usually the depleted energy reserves of the campers; in other words, their sloth level. People that have been paddling all day except when they are portaging, and who have been sleeping on the rocky ground for several days, are usually not inclined to start looking for appropriately placed trees that their common sense tells them don't exist in the first place. And, besides, if you've never had a bear in camp in the past, what's the problem? As a result, the food pack is frequently simply rolled up in a tarp and leaned against one of the sitting logs that surround the fire grate—that way the campers, seated in the tent, don't have to throw rocks too far in the hope of scaring any bears away.

The last night of a trip is always quiet and the campers are always reflective. Usually it's less than twenty-four hours from civilization and the campfire time is spent thinking about the last several days and nights. This particular last night was no different from any other last night for Rick, Dan and me. We had a small but adequate fire. I had spent the better part of an hour looking for campfire wood but all I could find was wood that burned, which is not necessarily the same thing. As we sat around the fire I thought it odd that this wood was not burning and not putting off as much heat as I thought it would, given how dry it was. Prior to dinner I walked deep behind the campsite in search of wood and everything was dry, dry, dry. And, because it was so dry, every step taken produced a loud "crack" or "snap" as my foot broke a downed branch or twig. The wild grass was yellow and dry. It had been an arid summer, and to my way of thinking, conditions seemed conducive for an uncontrolled forest fire.

So, after we had eaten, done the dishes, filled our water bottles and got the fire going, we had to deal with the food pack. The three of us had started three days earlier, and the last three nights had all been bear-free. Yes, we had been getting closer to Lake Polly—the enormous rock at the southern tip of Malberg Lake told us that—but when a person doesn't want to do something (like hang a food pack) a person can find lots of reasons not to do it. A person's mind is capable of great feats of rationalization that, upon reflection at a later date, turn out to be stupid decisions justified by unreasonable conclusions.

On this particular night we opted for the easy approach (i.e., the sloth approach). We rolled up the food pack in a blue tarp to keep out the mice and stashed it under the aluminum canoe (an aluminum canoe make lots of noise when it's pushed and pulled across rock). We were cognizant of the warnings about the Lake Polly Bear but it occurred to me that, as best as I could recall, no one had actually ever really *seen* the legendary bear. Oh, there were countless reports of missing food packs or shredded food packs, but never an actual, confirmed sighting of the raider bruin. I was beginning to think that the Lake Polly Bear was about as real as an alien abduction. Dan, who has done more canoe trips than me, and Rick, who was Dan's mentor, felt comfortable stashing the remains of our food under my seventeen-foot, sixty-seven-pound Grumman. Who was I to complain?

We let the fire slowly die on its own, and when it was out we went to bed. Dan and Rick shared one tent about forty feet north of the fire grate, and my tent was about forty feet east of the fire grate.

It's generally considered good advice to establish a pattern when camping, be it what to do, when to do it, how to do it and where to do it. If one has to get up in the middle of the night for whatever reason, it's helpful to know that one's headlamp is going to be in one place, one's water bottle is going to be in another place, one's shoes are going to be in yet another place, etc. That way, a person can find anything and everything in the dark. Some people are more organized than others, but even the most disorganized person must have some system for putting things away so that they can be easily located later. After I finished reading, I put my book in its usual place, got undressed, stashed my glasses, headlamp and shoes where I knew I could find them, blew out the candle and closed my eyes, knowing that Dan and Rick were doing just about the same thing.

Lots of things go "bump in the dark" when one is sleeping in a tent in the wilderness, but experienced campers have already learned that little things can make big noises when it's dark. And it helps to remind oneself that, aside from the rare psychotic wolverine, all of the animals in the forest have more to fear from humans than humans have to fear from the animals. Experienced campers learn to assume that the noises that they hear on the other side of the tent fabric, whatever they may be, are not harbingers of danger. In other words, the noises are ignored.

So, when I awoke a few hours later to a rustling in the bushes and shrubs, I reassured myself that it's probably a little mouse trying to make a living. It was even fun to listen to at first. But fun left the picture when I heard the branch break. Mice are usually seen before being heard, and there's no mouse heavy enough to break a branch.

"OK, so maybe that's not a mouse that I'm hearing," I said to myself.

Still not overly worried or concerned, I asked myself, "So what is it?"

Squirrels and chipmunks are bigger and heavier than mice and would surely make more noise, but it was 1:30 a.m. and all self-respecting squirrels and chipmunks were in bed, just like I was. And they were sleeping, which is what I no longer was.

In fact, I was no longer even close to sleeping. I was wide awake, nervous system overdosing on adrenalin, sitting up straight as a chair, trying to listen to what was going on outside of my tent, because the loud "crunch" that I had just heard was telling me that the animal moving around in the dark had some heft to it.

I ran down the list: deer (possible, but not a threat), psychotic wolverine (unlikely—I wasn't in Michigan), timber wolf (never—they avoid humans). What could it be?

What could it be?

Could it be?

Could it really be?

Could it really be the Lake Polly Bear?

I'm not sure what makes a person more vulnerable—being legally blind and not being able to find one's glasses, or being stark raving, absolutely bare ass (and I do mean bare ass) buck naked. But in my case the question was academic, because I couldn't find either my glasses or my underwear. And judging from the now enormous racket coming from just outside my tent, I had time for a few hurried breaths before I had my chips cashed in. I couldn't even find my headlamp, which was probably just as well. Knowing that I was about to die, I'm not sure if I really wanted to see the black claws of the Lake Polly Bear as it ripped my nylon tent wide open. I had read once that bears have notoriously bad breath, and I found myself wondering if bear breath would be the second to last thing to register in my brain— the last thing, of course, being my skin and flesh and arteries and red muscle mass and whatever little body fat I carried, all being savagely torn and shredded by a several-hundred-pound starving creature that was absolutely fed up with eating granola and dehydrated bananas.

In such moments panic develops, growing by leaps and bounds, rudely pushing aside the rational state of being until it takes charge of the situation, all in about a heartbeat of time. Sitting up straight, wide awake, eyes wide open, in my birthday suit, no glasses, no headlamp, no weapon of any kind, and with precious little time with which to review my sorry life or to even implore Divine Intervention, I did what I could.

What any terrified Homo sapiens in my situation would have done.

I screamed.

Loud.

AAAAAARRRRRRGGGGGGHHHHHH!!!!!

I couldn't believe it. I was alive.

I screamed again, only louder this time.

AAAAAARRRRRRGGGGGGHHHHHH!!!!!

I couldn't believe it. I was still alive.

I screamed a third time. Still louder.

AAAAAARRRRRRGGGGGGHHHHHH!!!!!

I couldn't believe it. I was *still* alive.

But I could scream no more.

Screaming at the top of one's lungs, filling one's lungs with as much air as one could, and then expelling it through one's mouth as powerfully as possible, plays havoc on the screamer's vocal chords.

It began to look as if I just might survive, but without a voice.

That's when I heard Dan.

As the Lake Polly Bear had been contemplating its flanking assault on my tent, Dan had heard the same rustle that I had heard. As the Lake Polly Bear had advanced toward its midnight snack (me!), Dan had gotten dressed. As the Lake Polly Bear got so close to my tent that I could have sworn that I saw its silhouette in the moonlight, Dan had put on his sandals, grabbed his headlamp and gone outside. And as the Lake Polly Bear had raised its right paw, extended its claws and lifted its chops, Dan yelled out, "I see it! I see it! It's a bea..."

An adult Castor canadensis is 90 to 117 centimeters long and weighs about 35 kilograms fully grown. For those of you not versed in the metric system, that's about 36 to 46 inches long and about 77 pounds heavy. It has a dark brown coat with long glossy guard hairs overlying a very dense, insulating undercoat. Razor-sharp incisors specially adapted to cut wood dominate the front of its mouth. But its most distinguishing feature is its tail. The tail of a Castor canadensis looks like a canoe paddle with the shaft missing.

I couldn't believe it. The Lake Polly Bear wasn't a bear at all. At least not this night it wasn't. The Lake Polly Bear was a beaver!

Without realizing it, we had set up our tents pretty close to a path that the resident beavers used as they waddled up the shore and into the brush to get wood. The beavers used the same path on their return to the water. It had been an arid summer, and all of the plants that were alive were dry. The dead plants were even drier. A seventy-seven-pound beaver, even if it is a vegetarian, makes a tremendously loud noise as it pushes its way through the dry grass, stepping on dead twigs and branches, all the while dragging a six-foot-long branch from a birch tree, especially when the person listening is without any glasses, clothes, shoes or headlamp and is sitting in a puddle of his own salty sweat.

Finding my glasses and underwear and shoes and headlamp was considerably easier than finding my composure, but after awhile I was fit to go out in public, or at least fit enough to crawl out of my tent and join Dan who was standing on the shore, watching the Lake Polly Beaver. Dan didn't say anything about my reaction, but I thought I saw a slight smile and a subtle shaking and dropping of his head as he stole a glance at his very recently terrorized, pathetic friend.

Rick apparently slept through the entire event.

Sure enough, there was the Lake Polly Beaver—swimming through the circles of light created by our headlamps. Beavers are supposed to be wild, but I thought that this one was swimming pretty close to us.

Perhaps it wanted to get a good look at the two humans that were camped next to its thoroughfare. Or perhaps it wanted to get a good sniff of the human that it had frightened almost to death. It swam so close to us that I could see it wiggling its nose. I thought about grabbing a rock and throwing it at the Lake Polly Beaver—I couldn't have missed it, it was so close—but I realized that it was not even two in the morning, and I still had to get back to sleep. The beaver had accidentally almost put me into cardiac arrest, and I didn't want to find out what a purposeful and vengeful beaver could do to me if it wanted to. I didn't want to be sleeping and have a 450-pound birch tree fall on my tent.

While Rick continued to sleep (there's something to be said for those that are not informed and unaware), Dan and I stoked the fire. We talked about this, that and the other thing until the fire died out and my adrenalin burned off and we went to bed.

I slept like a baby, in my underwear, with my shoes on my feet and my glasses and headlamp on my head.

SOME SAYINGS TO TRAVEL BY

What follows are some sayings or nuggets of advice that I have accumulated over the years—sitting around a campfire, reading a book, having lunch on a travelling day, attending a slide show, etc. I have repeated them just as I recall them. They all seem like good advice to me. I have named the source when available, although many of the sayings have passed into the public domain long ago.

In order to have good judgment you have to survive bad judgment.
—Unknown

I have found that people go to the wilderness for many things....
They go to the wilderness for the good of their souls.
—Sigurd Olson

Don't let the reasons for reaching your destination become more important than reaching your destination.
—Unknown

When packing for a trip: If you'll need it, bring it along.
If you might need it, leave it behind.
If you want it, bring it along (two items).
—Unknown

Mistakes multiply and accidents accumulate when you're in a hurry.
—Unknown

Play harder than you work.
—Unknown

Do not fight Nature, rather, accept it on friendly terms and deeply enjoy its variable moods.
—Calvin Rutstrum

You're here to have fun.
—Common Sense

OF WOMEN AND WOLVES

Everything seemed to happen in slow motion.

Had she taken the time to think about it, it would have made perfect sense. New experiences always seem to take longer. Things are drawn out. If one travels the same route to a familiar destination time and time again, any given day's trip is nothing but an ignored combination of sights and sounds and smells, and upon arriving one has difficulty recalling any particular details of what had just happened. The trip to wherever seems to take very little time at all. But if one takes a different route for the first time, everything is novel and one notices all of the little things that will soon be ignored when the new route becomes familiar and is taken for granted. When experiencing something new, time seems to slow down, as if to give one even more of an opportunity to experience the event. And the mind, which is fully capable of effortlessly ignoring the common, routine, pedestrian events of life, can all of a sudden turn into an empty sponge demanding data from eyes, ears and nose. At such times the mind cannot accumulate enough information. The mind becomes exceedingly sensitive and gathers in everything it can, to be sorted out later.

So it was with Boody. What had just happened to her had never happened to her before. It only took a matter of one or two seconds—no more than that—but in those few brief moments Boody was surprised by the sheer volume of things she had noticed. How it felt, what she had been thinking about when it happened, how things looked at the time, what the sounds were, the smell in the air, and just how utterly slow it took.

She had picked her route carefully, and she was enjoying her solitude as she started to ski across the frozen river. Boody loved being outside and she didn't need what most people consider to be nice weather to have a nice time. She was content with the gray overcast and the high teens temperature that the day had brought her. Bright blue sky and bright yellow sun weren't really necessary for Boody. She had been looking forward to an afternoon of exploring, and she knew that when she returned to camp all she would have to do would be to gather some more firewood and she'd be set for the evening.

She found herself wondering why she had not hollered out when it happened. It seemed to her that she would have had enough time to do so. One obvious reason was that she was alone and there simply was no one to holler to. But the primary reason why she had remained silent was much more abstract, much more unsettling and much more ominous. She didn't holler out because, in the few seconds that it had taken to happen, she was surprised to realize that, after all these years and all of her trips, it had finally happened to her.

"It," in general terms, meant an accident. But more specifically for Roberta Budrough "Boody" Leeds—age 26, single, shoulder-length red hair, born in Maine but raised and living in the Upper Peninsula, high school earth sciences teacher, accomplished cross-country skier, solo winter camper of considerable experience, lover of the outdoors, volunteer driver for Meals on Wheels, solid neighbor but behind on her credit card payments, owner of two Malamutes and a cat named Jiggles—"it" meant punching through the thin layer of ice on a river that, in the middle, which is where she had been skiing, was more than two feet deeper than she was tall.

There had been very little noise. As accidents happen, this had been a quiet one. There had been no sound at all as Boody's skis broke through the thin layer of ice. There had been a slight, muffled gurgling sound as she sank into the cold water, first skis, then boots, then shins, then knees, then thighs, then her crotch, quickly followed by her waist and her chest, and finally, the tops of her shoulders. Boody dropped her ski poles, and they landed nearby. She managed to get her elbows on top of the ice and hold her head out of the water.

Boody had originally sank until the tops of her shoulders were below the surface of the water, but she had dressed in layers, and the layers of clothing that she had been wearing now acted as a barrier, keeping the cold water at bay, while at the same time trapping the air close to her body, providing buoyancy.

Boody bobbed up and down on the surface and took stock of her situation. She was alone, about two miles from her camp, floating in ice cold water that splashed across her shoulders and onto her angular face on a late Tuesday afternoon following a bitterly cold Monday evening in early February. She noticed that, just a few seconds ago, she had been floating a bit higher, but the cold water had been busy, first searching out the pockets of warm air trapped between her layers of clothing, and then, after finding the pockets of air that were holding her up, slowly forcing the air out through her neck and the bottoms of her sleeves and the bottom of her upper underwear and wind jacket and even through the fabric itself.

Boody knew that the water was cold—some had splashed on her face as her shoulders had submerged—but after several seconds Boody began to realize just how cold the water really was. She felt the cold water on her thighs and chest, but not as much as she felt the cold water on her fingers. All she had been wearing on her hands were very thin polypropylene liner gloves. Boody noticed that the small of her back was still somewhat dry and her feet, protected by her ski boots and two pairs of socks and tied off by her laces, were still bone dry.

Boody's personality, if one would attempt to describe it, would best be summed up as finding humor in any situation. But Boody now found herself in new territory; territory that her personality had not yet experienced. She knew, intellectually, that she was in a lot of trouble and that the odds of getting out of it were not good. Emotionally, she was still wrestling with the fact that, after so many years of solo tripping, she had finally become "one of them." One of them, of course, being the other people that bad things always seemed to happen to.

After a few more seconds, which was about as long as it took for Boody to realize that she had to do something, the small of her back had filled with the cold water and the last pockets of air between her underwear and her wind suit had been purged. And now, she was floating even lower in the water—the cold water was above her shoulders again. And her clothes, now soaked with the cold water, were making it difficult for her to move.

The hole in the ice that Boody found herself in was about six feet long by about two and a half feet wide. The ice surrounding the hole appeared to be about two inches thick—certainly thick enough to support Boody, if only she could get up on top of it. Boody was wondering how it was that she had broken through the ice in the first place. She had been careful in picking her spot to cross and had not noticed anything to suggest that the ice might be too thin to support her. Had the sun been shining the contrast would have been greater and Boody might have noticed the slight discoloration in the snow about twenty-five feet in front of her as she began crossing the frozen river. But exactly how it had happened was a luxury that Boody couldn't afford to think about presently; right now she was about to start the fight of her life, and she knew it. She also believed, on an instinctive level, that because she was alone, soaking wet and two miles away from her camp on a cold winter day, that even if she did somehow manage to pull herself out of the hole in the ice, by the end of this day, she would be dead.

The first thing she had to do was to get out of the hole. She put one arm atop the ice first, followed by the other arm, but the change in Boody's center of gravity pushed her even deeper into the now possessive cold water, cold water that Boody knew would not release her willingly. Boody tried kicking her feet and suddenly remembered that she still had her skis on. Boody knew that her skis would have to come off.

Getting her skis off would normally not be difficult—Boody did it all the time. Standing on a ski trail, all she usually had to do was push the tip of her ski pole into the release mechanism and the mechanism would open, the ski would come off, and she could then remove the other ski. But both skis were under water, and although her poles were within reach near the hole, Boody knew that she would never be able to get her skis off with her ski pole. Boody realized that only way to remove her skis would be to reach down with her right arm while pulling up her right leg. She would have to push the release mechanism with her now nearly frozen fingers.

Boody reached down with her arm while pulling up her leg. But the change in the center of gravity pulled Boody's head under water, and now her dunking was complete. Her submerging was something that Boody had not anticipated, and she ended up with her head below the surface and a mouthful of ice water. Boody fought her way back to the surface, emptied her mouth, and for the first time, felt panic.

Boody reached down a second time, submerged a second time, rose to the surface a second time and emptied her mouth again. She continued to try and try, and after what must have been the sixth or seventh attempt she was able to find the release mechanism with the now stinging fingers of her right hand. Boody pushed against the release mechanism—and nothing happened. Boody now regretted not oiling the release mechanism as she had intended for several weeks.

Several more attempts lead to Boody being submerged several more times, but she was eventually able to reach down, find the release mechanism, and while holding her right foot steady, open the release mechanism, allowing the ski to separate from the binding and float to the surface.

The left ski came off with a bit less effort but Boody was now chilled to the bone. She knew that, physically, she was in good shape but nevertheless she was exhausted.

Next, Boody had to get out the water. She tried several times to get atop the ice, but the only thing she could do was keep both elbows on top of the ice, and she propped herself up as best as she could. She tried kicking with her feet but her legs were heavy, weighted down by her wet clothing and her boots, which were now finally beginning to take on water. She needed something sharp, something that she could poke into the ice that would not slip or slide, and she found what she needed in the dagger points of her ski poles.

Boody grabbed each pole by its basket, leaving the pointed ends exposed. She stabbed the first pole into the ice with her right hand, and then, reaching beyond the pole in her right hand, she stuck the other pole down with her left hand. She pulled as hard as she could, and she came ever so slightly out of the water. Boody then reached beyond her left hand and, with her right hand, again stabbed the first pole down, about another six inches beyond. She pulled again as hard as she could and a little bit more of her torso rose from the cold, slushy water. Boody repeated the process time and time again, and each time a little more of her body emerged, until finally her waist, then her seat, her thighs, her knees, her shins and, finally, her feet were all out of the water. Boody slithered on her stomach away from the hole in the ice until she was kneeling at the shoreline. She was cold, exhausted and frightened.

She didn't know how long she had been in the water, but she noticed that the sun was sinking toward the horizon, and she knew that the temperature was also falling just as fast. Last night had been a cold one—twelve degrees below zero—and Boody knew that tonight would be just as cold. Boody rolled in the snow, hoping that the powder would absorb most of the cold water on her wind suit, but the temperature was already so low that her wind suit was already freezing, and there was little cold water for the powder to absorb.

The pack that Boody had been carrying was still on her back. Inside the pack were food, fire starter and some matches. She used her teeth to pull her rapidly freezing gloves off of her hands. She fumbled for the zipper with her numbing fingers, forcing herself to guide her fingers by sight alone, her fingers already too dead to distinguish any feeling. She managed to grasp one of the zipper pulls but found that, as hard as she tugged, the zipper pull would not move. And then she saw why: when Boody went through the ice and into the cold water, her pack got wet. The zipper had become soaked with cold water, and now that the pack was exposed to the cold air, the cold water on the zipper froze. The pack could not be opened until it thawed. While she was preoccupied with her pack, Boody didn't notice that it had started to snow.

Boody forced her confused mind to review her options, which weren't many. She knew that she couldn't open her pack to retrieve the fire starter and matches, and she knew that she couldn't start a fire by friction. Her only chance was to get back to her camp. It was then that Boody hollered, but her cry for help was just as likely not to be heard then than if she had cried out for help when she first fell through the ice.

Believing that the effort would be futile, Boody nevertheless decided to try to get back to her camp, which was located about two miles away. Knowing that she could ski faster than she could walk, she realized that she would need her skis. She crawled back as close to the hole in the ice as she dared and hooked the binding of each ski with the straps of her ski poles. She pulled her skis out of the water and then crawled back to shore, pushing the skis before her. When she got back to shore she stood up and tried putting her skis on. But when Boody fell through the ice, her ski bindings got wet. While the bindings were still in the cold water, Boody had been able to open both of them with considerable effort. But her wet bindings had, just like the zipper on the backpack, now been exposed to the freezing air. And her bindings, just like the zipper on her backpack, were now frozen solid and would have to be thawed before they could be used. Overcome with frustration, Boody threw her ski into the air. She didn't even bother to try the other binding.

Boody started stumbling the two miles back to her camp on feet that were wet and close to freezing. She checked the little thermometer that was fastened to the strap on one of her ski poles—it was only three degrees above zero. Her wind suit was starting to freeze along its crease lines and whenever Boody made an awkward movement—which was often—little bits of ice would break off and fall into the snow. She no longer had feeling in her fingers. Even the stinging pain of cold fingers being warmed would have been welcome, but there was nothing. Boody knew that she had come down the west shore of the frozen river but on her return found it difficult to find her tracks. It was then that Boody noticed it was snowing. She didn't have to follow her tracks to find her camp, but the sight of the earlier tracks would have been reassuring. As it was, she had nothing to reassure her, and she began to weep.

Boody's strides, never long to begin with, had begun to shrink. She found that she was using more and more of her limited energy in taking one step after another. Boody stopped to rest frequently, maybe as many as a dozen times, and felt that she must be getting close to her camp. But when she turned around to check on her progress, she was crushed to see that she had traveled at most only two hundred yards. Boody could still see one of her skis standing up, tangled in a downed spruce tree where it had landed after she threw it.

Boody found herself no longer taking steps with both feet; rather, she would take one step with her left foot—about twelve inches long—and then drag her right foot forward. Soon she found that she no longer had the energy to pick her left foot up at all. She simply dragged one foot after the other. It was only a matter of time before she could no longer even do that.

At some point—Boody didn't realize when—she had fallen and now found herself on her hands and knees, too exhausted to cry but too frightened not to try to get back up. She tried to struggle to her feet and found that she could not get up. Remembering that she had dragged herself out of the hole in the ice, she tried dragging herself along the trail on her elbows but could make no progress at all. Her elbows dug into the soft snow, but Boody no longer had the energy to pull. Refusing to give up, she tried crawling while laying flat on the ground, but Boody was no longer able to control her legs.

Without realizing it, Boody had been drifting in and out of consciousness. She no longer was aware that she couldn't move. She continued to try to move her legs but accomplished little more than occasionally twitching, first one leg and then the other. Had she been aware, she would have realized that the twitches in her legs were numbering fewer and fewer, and the time between each was lengthening. After awhile, Boody stopped moving entirely, except for her labored breathing. And, after awhile, that stopped too.

But just before her breathing stopped entirely, Boody looked up and thought she saw in the gathering dusk the outline of an animal that appeared to be slowly approaching her, its head down, its ears up, its eyes sharp black points staring into her own. Boody lay down her head and lay still, and she accepted the inevitable surrender to the cold. The falling snow quietly started to accumulate, filling in around her knees and elbows and covering her frozen red hair that stuck out from beneath her hat, until finally, Boody's body from a distance looked like a snow-covered rock.

The alpha male had become confused trying to obey its conflicting instincts. Its ultrafine sense of smell had earlier detected the repugnant odor of its one and only enemy in the north woods—a human being—and its survival instinct told it to turn and trot away. But its sixth sense had detected something else on the teasing wind currents. It had detected the scent of fear. The phantom of the north forest was compelled forward, its sense of curiosity overcoming its fear of the human. The timber wolf had been watching Boody, the source of the repugnant odor and the source of the scent of fear, in her death throes for several minutes. The timber wolf had watched Boody's death struggle with seeming indifference. Centuries of breeding and imprinting had given the timber wolf keen instincts that it would need to survive, and it instinctively knew that the human it had been watching was about to die. But, lacking self-awareness, the wild beast was unable to comprehend what death meant.

The timber wolf waited for several more minutes after Boody stopped moving before it trotted out from behind a downed tree and took several measured steps towards the snow-covered lump on the ice, all the while ever alert and vigilant, its hackles standing up on end, its nose to the ground, its ears up, its eyes fixated on the still and motionless human. The timber wolf saw the human raise its head but instinctively knew that the human was no longer a threat. It paused, then waited, and then proceeded several more paces until it was about twenty-five feet away from the human. It sniffed the air and recognized the unmistakable scent of death.

It would not be inaccurate to say that the timber wolf remembered when it had fallen through the ice a few years earlier, but to attribute to the timber wolf human emotions and mental capabilities beyond that would be improper. The timber wolf, although capable of learning lessons from its own mistakes, was a beast of instinct. When the timber wolf had fallen through the ice, it instinctively knew that it had to swim to get out, for the water was deeper than it could hold its head above.

The timber wolf's experience had been similar to Boody's. It had been crossing a snow-covered river that its instincts had suggested was safe to cross. But as all experienced human winter travelers know, sometimes there are thin spots of ice that cannot be accounted for. There are no visible rocks to disrupt the current, and there are no obvious ice shelves that would suggest that the path might not be safe. There are no bends or curves in the river. These thin spots of ice, sometimes known as "wild cards," appear fortunately infrequently, but when they appear they appear without notice. Such was Boody's experience, as it had been the timber wolf's.

When the timber wolf fell through the ice it had no hope of climbing out. A timber wolf does not carry ice picks and would not know how to use a ski pole as a tool. But the timber wolf instinctively knew that its only hope to get out was to swim to the edge of the hole, push its chest against the ice, and kick with its feet. And that's what the timber wolf did. Had the ice been any thicker than it had been, the timber wolf would have failed. But the ice was thin enough for the timber wolf to plow through, and much like an icebreaker on the Great Lakes, the timber wolf continuously pushed the tops of its shoulders against the thin ice while kicking with all of its feet until it had broken a path through the ice to a point close enough to shore so that it could finally stand on the river bed and climb out.

Cold and soaked, it shivered and shook as its body shed what water it could, all the while internally generating heat to warm itself, until it was warm enough to move on. The timber wolf had instinctively known which direction to try and break the ice with its chest, and the path it had chosen that day was not the shortest path to the shore. Had the timber wolf gone directly toward shore, the ice would have been too thick to push through, and like Boody, it would have died, claimed by one of Nature's innumerable winter rivers.

Experienced pilots and experienced sailors, like experienced people who travel the wilderness, have learned, usually through trial and error, that Nature does not object to its being used and traveled through and enjoyed, but Nature is also completely indifferent to the perils of those that find themselves in danger, be it by accident, negligence or carelessness. Nature doesn't care how its visitors get into trouble, and Nature does not help them out of whatever troubles its visitors might find themselves in.

The wolf survived.

Boody did not.

Five months to the day after Boody froze to death on the shore of a river in the wilderness, two men were fishing for walleye on a day trip away from their base camp. To get from the lake they were camped on to the lake that they wanted to fish, they had to paddle a three-quarter-mile-long unnamed river. While paddling down the river, the bowman noticed a cross-country ski tangled in a dead spruce that had toppled over and was leaning in the water. Close by they found the second ski, and about thirty yards from the first ski they found a ski pole. They brought all three back to their camp where they examined their find more closely. There, on a sticker on each of the two skis was the name: Boody Leeds.

The Forest Service was notified, and it dispatched several two-person canoe teams to search the river and adjoining lakes. One of the canoe teams found the tattered remnants of a supplex nylon wind suit. Now confident that it had found the general area where Boody Leeds was forever resting, the Forest Service concentrated its search on the river, hoping to find human remains. But it had been five months since Boody had disappeared, and in spite of the efforts of the Forest Service and several of Boody's friends who volunteered to help with the search, no further sign of Boody Leeds was ever found.

And knowledge of her ultimate fate is to this day unknown by humans.

The alpha male that had witnessed Boody's introduction to death was the leader of a pack of nine timber wolves. It had responsibilities of its own, although it certainly could not understand them as such. To the alpha male, Boody's body represented nourishment for its pack. Late in the evening on the day of Boody's death, the alpha male howled a command to its pack to assemble at the north end of the river. Individual timber wolves appeared, as did two pair, until the eight lesser timber wolves came together in the presence of their leader. The alpha male led them to Boody's body.

In spite of the fact that Boody represented the timber wolves' sole enemy in the north woods, the timber wolves that satisfied their hunger did so without animosity or revenge. The beasts were incapable of experiencing such emotions in any event. Because animals are believed to be devoid of complex emotions or even simple awareness, they are considered to be inferior to humans. Much has been written about the moral superiority of the human race, about its accomplishments in establishing order, in its appreciation of music, art and poetry, in its establishment of religion, in its recognition of an individual's personal rights, in its engineering triumphs and in its social concern for the less fortunate. On the other hand, animals have never been known to practice genocide on a scale that measured in the millions, or to make organized war, or to torture with pleasure, or to waste resources, or to brag about their successes or to flaunt their abilities. Animals certainly do kill one another to be sure, but many also spend their time as parents caring for their young, and they do so without complaint.

Roberta Budrough "Boody" Leeds, for her last vision in life, saw the alpha male slowly approaching her. She knew what would certainly happen to her body. Roberta Budrough "Boody" Leeds, high school earth sciences teacher, accomplished cross-country skier, solo winter camper of considerable experience, a lover of the outdoors, the owner of two Malamutes and a cat named Jiggles, would not have objected to her ultimate fate.

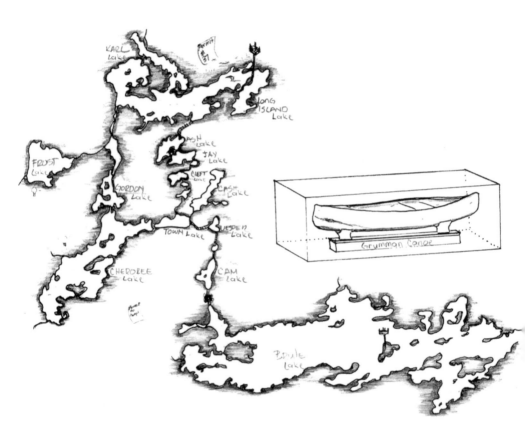

BOUNDARY WATERS CAMPING IN THE 22ND CENTURY

Conner and Judy were ecstatic.

Their long anticipated canoe trip was about to begin.

Conner had begun planning this trip by applying for a permit seven years ago when he and his then wife Lisa returned from their last canoe trip—four days and three nights out of Ely. The Ely trip had been Conner's fourth time into the half-million-acre Boundary Waters Canoe and Motorboat Recreational Area. Conner had especially enjoyed Ely, a bustling city of eleven thousand people that still retained some "small-town" flavor. Conner remembered how privileged he had felt on that trip; it had been his fourth canoe camping trip in his then thirty-seven years. The competition for permits had become so fierce that Conner knew people and had friends who had only been able to manage two or three canoe trips by the time they were forty. And here was Conner, now forty-four years old, about to embark on this, his *fifth* canoe trip. A lucky man indeed, he felt himself to be.

Wilderness areas dwindling in size and numbers, soaring numbers of campers, butchered budgets and federal and state government policies encouraging development had required the Department of Agriculture and Internal Security to make significant changes in how it managed the Boundary Waters Canoe and Motorboat Recreational Area. There had been a time around the turn of the century when the old Boundary Waters Canoe Area Wilderness (BWCAW), the predecessor to today's Recreational Area, had been a full one million acres in size with two thousand campsites, when groups of nine could enter and stay as long as they wanted, when Ely had a population of five thousand and when there was no nickel mining industry in northern Minnesota.

But that was now well over a hundred years ago, and Conner knew that changes had to have been made to meet the ever-increasing demands on the country's resources. The first major change that affected the old BWCAW had been the National Omnibus Wilderness and Natural Resources Act of 2027, or more simply known as the "2027 Act." This legislation had been instrumental in opening up for development what had been the old BWCAW. The discovery of more economical ways to mine and process nickel meant that Minnesota's large nickel deposits would be ignored no longer.

The legislation decreased, or "rolled back," the size of the old BWCAW in incremental steps every ten years. When the rollback had begun, the BWCAW had consisted of about one million acres in three separate parts. The final adjustment was due in 2110—only three years away—and would leave the Boundary Waters Canoe and Motorboat Recreational Area officially at 497,643 acres in one large tract. The part of the old BWCAW that had extended east from the Gunflint Trail had disappeared with the adjustments of 2060, and the western part of the old BWCAW had been swallowed up when Highway 1 was extended from Ely to International Falls in 2080. The two-lane bridge across Burntside Lake was generally considered to be an eyesore, but people driving to the border appreciated the hour that the bridge and highway saved them. The "169ers," named for the highway that they preferred, had fought the bridge and highway, to no avail.

Slowly but surely, at the end of each decade the BWCAW borders had been rolled back to ensure that the nickel industry would not run out of land to mine. It seemed that the farther east one explored, the more nickel one found, and the quicker the old BWCAW had shrunk. The legislation that permitted the continuous scaling back of the wilderness had been controversial at the time and had been bitterly opposed by environmentalists, and there had even been some sporadic incidents of violence and vandalism, but promises of jobs, better wages and freedom from dependence of foreign sources of nickel had won out, as they invariably do. Slowly but surely the wilderness began to shrink, while cities like Ely and Babbitt began to grow. Babbitt was now called home by 9,500 people and was the county seat of North

St. Louis County. Establishment of the county seat in Minnesota's 88th county had been a mean and vicious battle between Babbitt and Hibbing, but ultimately it was felt that the seat of the new county should be close to the reason for splitting up the old St. Louis County in the first place. Taconite was out, nickel was in and Babbitt won.

In 2050, Congress enacted the National Wilderness and Recreational Lands Reconciliation Act, which reclassified many publicly owned tracts of land. The major and traditional favorite places, such as Yosemite, Yellowstone and Glacier National Parks, had survived without much change at all, but other areas, such as the BWCAW, suffered major restructuring. President Hernandez had vetoed the legislation, but in that era of development for development's sake, environmental issues had taken a backseat to proposals and plans to develop undeveloped areas, and her veto had been overridden by Congress. The National Wilderness and Recreational Lands Reconciliation Act became known as the "Wild to Mild" law. In the case of the old BWCAW, the Wild to Mild law permitted boats and motors on any lake to which the boat's owner could get it, provided that the motor's horsepower was limited to two hundred. In the process the old BWCAW officially became known as the Boundary Waters Canoe and Motorboat Recreational Area.

Conner found it amusing that during the seven years it had taken him to get a permit for this trip, he had had the time to become a father, divorce Lisa, meet and marry Judy. And now, here he was, adjusting the magnets to keep his eighteen-pound canoe on the top of his electrovan. Conner had studied the map of his trip and knew that there were some portages that he'd have to carry his canoe over, and he wondered how people used to portage the heavier canoes of one hundred years ago—the big forty-five-pound Kevlar boats.

As he made the final adjustments to the magnets, he promised himself to show Judy the aluminum canoe on display in the Dorothy Molter Museum in Ely. That canoe was an ancient Grumman, not a standard Grumman but a lighter-weight version that still tipped the scales at a full sixty-seven pounds of aluminum. It had a hull marred by scars and pits and a wicked four-foot-long gouge—evidence of an encounter with a submerged rock. On the bow there was a chipped and faded, but still very easily recognized, outline of a black star, probably put there by a previous owner, for reasons never to be known.

As Conner made the final adjustments to the van and canoe his six-year-old daughter DebAnn came up to him and, for what must have been the thousandth time, asked where they were going. Conner explained that for DebAnn's first camping trip they would insert the electrovan into the electric-powered traffic flow lane from Minneapolis up the interstate to Duluth, where they would spend the night with grandma. From Duluth they would take the four-lane expressway all the way to Tofte, and from there they would take the three-lane blacktop Sawbill Trail all the way to another asphalt road known for as long as anyone could remember simply as "The Grade." They would drive east, then north, and ultimately arrive at Brule Lake, where they had reservations at the Brule Lake Inn. From the Brule Lake Inn they would take the ferry across Brule Lake to the western shore and dock at the portage to Cam Lake. Once tied up, the ferry would unload Conner, Judy, DebAnn and DebAnn's friend Cindy and thirty-six other people, representing ten separate camping groups. The ferry would leave about three hours later, returning forty outgoing campers to the Brule Lake Inn. From Cam Lake Conner and his group would head north with their assigned guide to Long Island Lake and Site #37, the lake and site that had been randomly assigned to Conner in the lottery for a permit.

In a desperate attempt to preserve the quality of the campsites in the canoe wilderness the Forest Service had decreased the maximum number of people per group while at the same time keeping the number of campsites intact at two thousand. The most recent reduction, in 2097, had decreased the maximum number of people per group from six to five, and Conner had learned that in the ten years since the reduction, many of the two thousand campsites had, indeed, started to recover from overuse. On the other hand, maintaining two thousand campsites in an area that was shrinking significantly in size every ten years meant overcrowding, and lakes that used to have four or five campsites frequently now had twenty.

For many years an unremarkable destination, Long Island Lake had become the third most popular entry point in what used to be the old BWCAW, and Conner fully expected to see motorboats on their trip. One of the things the 2027 Act had succeeded in doing was getting portage wheels back on the portages. The earlier portage wheels, which relied on people pulling and pushing their fishing boats, had been replaced, first by gas-powered engines and then ultimately by electrical-powered carts on twin rails, much like a miniature railroad. The extension of the electric grid into the Boundary Waters Canoe and Motorboat Recreational Area meant that there would be no need for internal combustion engines on the portages, or so the electrical industry had argued when it successfully lobbied the Department of Agriculture and Internal Security to allow the extension of electricity so that the year-round cabins on Cherokee Lake and Frost Lake would have power.

Conner continued to check his documentation, just to make sure that he had everything. Permit, reservation confirmation, passports, and North American Continent travel visas were all in order. The background checks had taken longer than they should have, but when one is travelling within fifty miles of any border that the United States shares with Canada, Mexico or California, a person must have in their possession under penalty of immediate incarceration and without due process, a laser/DNA scan identification vial and background clearance, and both had only just arrived.

About forty-eight hours later Conner found himself disengaging from the electric-powered traffic flow lane and he manually controlled the electrovan the last few miles to his mother's home in Duluth, where they spent the night. The next morning Conner drove to Brule Lake and the Brule Lake Inn. As they passed the Homer Lake Condominiums DebAnn asked her father if he thought if they'd catch any fish. Knowing that the public fishing pool at the Brule Lake Inn was regularly stocked with healthy game fish, Conner told his daughter that she'd be sure to catch a fish. Conner also knew that any fish that they caught while at Long Island Lake would have to be returned to the lake, the potential for mercury poisoning being far too great to justify the risk, but he didn't tell that to DebAnn.

Prior to checking out of the Brule Lake Inn the next day, Conner and Judy played the back nine at Eagle Mountain, and then Conner met their federally-mandated guide, Erin. The mandatory guide program was another one of those programs that was misguided or enlightened, depending on your point of view. On the one hand, being required to travel with a guide seemed to take much of the fun out of going in the first place for some people, but on the other hand, it was a guaranteed way for the Department of Agriculture and Internal Security to make sure that campers went where they were supposed to and stayed there. The mandatory guide program had been around for about forty-five years now and showed no sign of going away.

Erin brought them to the Forest Service check-in center, where, as at all other entry points, Forest Service personnel searched packs, bags and even the campers themselves for items that had been declared as illegal for possession in the Recreational Area: primarily bottles and cans, but now also firearms and knives with a blade longer than six inches. Finding nothing objectionable, the Forest Service waived Conner and his group through the check-in center, and they were led by Erin to their ferry, the *Tuscarora*. The *Tuscarora* was one of three ferries that served Brule Lake. Its sister ferry, the *Lake Saganaga* or *Big Sag* or even *the Sag*, plied the waters along the route to and from the Brule Lake Inn to South Cone Lake, whereas yet another sister ferry, the *Northern Lights*, carried campers and their gear to the eastern shore of Brule Lake.

By 2:30 on Tuesday afternoon Conner, Judy, DebAnn and DebAnn's friend Cindy and their guide Erin arrived at their designated campsite, Long Island Lake #37. It had a fire grate, a picnic table, an enclosed, heated latrine, two tent pads that were required to be used, a permanently installed pump for getting water out of the lake, a total and absolute prohibition against cutting any wood for fires, enough artificial wood to last for a week and, like every other of the two thousand campsites in the Boundary Waters Canoe and Motorboat Recreational Area, an emergency videophone and infrared Internet access. The tower on the large island in the middle of the lake guaranteed excellent reception. This site would be home for the next four nights. Conner was glad that he paid the extra twenty-five percent premium to extend their stay by another night. The restrictions on their permit prohibited any movement from Long Island Lake to another lake or river during their stay unless they obtained prior approval from the Long Island Lake District Management Office. That office was located about a quarter mile south of Site #37 and was staffed eight hours a day, and weather permitting, Conner would think about asking for permission to paddle up the river to Ham Lake.

While Conner and Erin set up their tents on the mandatory tent pads, Judy, DebAnn and Cindy went for a walk on the *Carbonfiber®* pathway that connected all seventeen sites on the western shore of Long Island Lake. Conner and Judy had had second thoughts about bringing DebAnn on the trip because of some fears she had expressed. Six-year-old DebAnn had been worried about being bitten by a wolf, but Conner assured her that there were no wild wolves any-more, at least not in Minnesota. After management of the Eastern Timber Wolf had been turned over by the federal government to the states once and for all in 2017, a series of misguided decisions (or enlightened decisions, again depending on the individual's value sys-tem) by state officials all but decimated the wolf population. Now, the closest pack of wild timber wolves in the lower forty-seven was in northern Wisconsin. After being reassured, DebAnn seemed to settle down and even started looking forward to the trip after Conner and Judy had shown her a picture of a loon and told her that she might actually see a live loon. During their walk DebAnn kept asking Judy if she had seen any loons yet. Judy had never seen a loon before either but didn't tell DebAnn that.

Although they were canoe camping in a water-dominated environ-ment, there were very few mosquitoes thanks to, or in spite of, efforts of the Forest Service to make the area more enjoyable. Advances in chemical engineering had produced pesticides that suppressed par-ticular species of insects, and the pesticides had been in use for over thirty years without noticeable changes to the general environment, although debate still continued as to the cause of dramatically increased rates of cancer among the residents of Lake, Cook and Northern St. Louis counties.

Conner, Judy, DebAnn and Cindy enjoyed their time at Site #37. The occasional powerboats towing water-skiers were not so numerous as to be annoying. Conner had attempted to get permission for a day trip to Ham Lake, but Forest Service staff had already granted permission to nine other parties to make the trip on that day, and it was felt that permitting another party would have been excessive. So, Conner's request had been denied. The girls thought the twinkle of the camp-fires all around the lake in the evening was pretty. At night they cooked marshmallows over the fire while their guide Erin told stories, not about animals or legends but rather about how people used to enjoy the canoe country one hundred years ago when her great-grandfather was a well-known guide for a well-known outfitter in Ely. Erin's great-grandfather had been a guide back in the days of the old BWCAW, and in his later years he had tried to instill in his descendants an appreciation of the old Boundary Waters as it used to be. Erin was a good and true steward of her great-grandfather's memories, but the area had changed so much that all Erin could do was preserve the sto-ries, never to have a chance herself to personally experience those long ago days.

On the evening before the day they were to leave, DebAnn and Judy saw their loon! Each evening at about ten o'clock the campers on the western end of Long Island Lake had heard the now unfamil-iar but once-upon-a-time signature sound of the old Boundary Waters Canoe Area Wilderness—the haunting wail of the common loon. Development of the area had wreaked havoc on the loons' breeding grounds until the state bird of Minnesota had all but disappeared. Occasional sightings of loons were reported, but for people who may only get to the Boundary Waters Canoe and Motorboat Recreational Area once or twice in their lives, there wasn't much of an opportuni-ty to see them. There had been talk of a loon family on Long Island Lake, but because there had been no sightings, people assumed that that's all it had been, talk. But on this night, DebAnn and Judy were on their nightly walk on the *Carbonfiber*® pathway that encircled the lake when they heard that unforgettable wail, and it was loud and close. They both stepped off the plastic path and walked about fifty yards until they reached a small point that partially sheltered a small bay. And, there it was: a large black and white waterbird, riding low in the water, with a red eye.

On the way out from Long Island Lake, Conner, Judy, DebAnn, Cindy and thirty-six other campers met a group of forty campers on their way in. That night they stayed at the Brule Lake Inn, and DebAnn got a chance to catch her fish from the public fishing pool.

On the drive home, Conner found himself thinking about their trip and his conversations with Erin. Conner found himself wondering what it must have been like a hundred years ago, or for that matter even earlier, when permits could be obtained on the day of one's trip, or an even earlier time when permits were not needed at all, when packs were not searched prior to entry into the wilderness, when campers could come and go when and where they pleased, when there were no enclosed latrines but there were mosquitoes, there were no picnic tables but there were fish safe to eat and seventy-five-pound canoes, when there were no telephones and transmission towers and when there was no artificial wood either, but when there were loons. He promised himself that he would begin the permit application process for another trip just as soon as they got home. With luck, they might be able to return before six-year-old DebAnn turned sixteen.

SLAUGHTER ON BIG SAG

Even from the get-go, there was something about this trip that was off. Something was not right. Maybe it was me.

On the final night of last September's season-ending canoe trip, six of us huddled shoulder to shoulder around a smoldering, anemic campfire in the chilly, deepening dusk and began planning this year's ambitious paddle: putting in at Saganaga Lake and cruising up the Voyageurs' Highway to Moose Lake—a route known by heart to the voyageurs of old. Four of us had Saganaga experience and were all too familiar with Sag's strong winds and challenging waves. Rumors of Saganaga near-death experiences rival those of Brule Lake, and that's saying something. Everyone said they were interested but I felt the commitment that they had always extended just wasn't there. People seemed to not be themselves. They were standoffish. Why were they ganging up against me? The following day we parted and went six different ways.

During the doldrums of the fall and winter months we kept in touch, picked our entry date and applied for our permit. As our departure date approached we started to divide the gear assignments among us—who would be responsible for bringing the canoes, who'd be driving, who'd be responsible for the food and figuring out who would bring the other group gear. In years past everyone looked forward to staying in touch with one another by email, and we'd make friendly challenges and tease each other about earlier mistakes and blunders we had all been guilty of. Those were the ways of six friends that had often traveled together. But the uncomfortable feelings left over from last year's trip carried over into the email conversations of the off-season months. Several responses to my emails were terse and several of my emails were simply ignored. Walt had been businesslike and impersonal. Something was definitely wrong, and I was going to get to the bottom of it.

September finally arrived, and the day before we were to put in on Sag we met up at Jim's place to review all of our gear. As soon as we got together it was obvious that there was still something going on. There was animosity in the air and nobody, especially Walt, seemed very friendly with anybody else, especially me. Just before leaving town, Matt, who had been my driving and paddling partner for years, surprised me by saying that he wanted to ride with Jim instead. The others couldn't help but notice, and I was insulted. Walt, saying little to anyone, had Dick join him and led our caravan of three pickups and canoes, with Matt and Jim second and Mark riding with me in the last truck. Mark seemed quiet and reserved and said little.

Our plan had us spending the night in the Trails End Campground at the end of the Gunflint Trail, and we stopped to eat on the way. As usual, the food was great, but it was a troubled dinner nonetheless, and my suspicion that something was wrong was confirmed when Walt and Matt got into an argument about politics. Walt seemed mad at the whole world. Both of them raised their voices, and our table started to draw stares and looks from diners at other tables who were trying to mind their own business but no longer could. After we left the restaurant and stood in the parking lot, Walt and Matt didn't say another word to each other.

"Well," I thought to myself, "Matt is yet another person who Walt couldn't get along with tonight."

I turned to Dick, but before I could say a word, he glared at me and walked away. What was going on? Walt, Matt, and Dick had all been rude to me today, and I was angry. We finished rounding out our plans as best we could and then headed to the end of the Gunflint Trail.

Arriving at the campground, we set up our tents and got a fire going. Sitting around the campfire, Walt and Matt picked up their argument where they had left off, and the two of them went at it, the argument being fueled by more beer. For a while I thought that things were going to get physical, and I saw that when Walt put his hand on the butt of the knife in his belt, Matt didn't back down. Walt and Matt had gotten along all right in the past, but there was no love lost between them tonight. Jim, usually easy and outgoing by nature, had been a model sphinx for the entire evening, except for when he told me to mind my own business after I had asked him about the bad feelings I had.

We got on the water at eight o'clock the next morning, with Walt and Dick in the first canoe. Surprisingly, Matt now said that he had changed his mind and he wanted to paddle with me. Over the last year Matt had been cold to me, and just yesterday he got into Jim's truck instead of mine, and now today, only twenty-four hours later, here he was in the bow of my canoe. Matt had insulted me yesterday, and now he was pretending that nothing had happened.

I decided to do something about it once we got on the water, and I knew what I was going to do. Matt needed a little excitement in his life. I didn't know what I was going to do about the others. I handed Matt a life vest after making some adjustments to it. I knew that Matt wasn't much of a swimmer, but the life vest was a self-inflating model, complete with CO_2 cartridge, and I knew that if Matt went in the water and if the self-inflating mechanism worked properly, Matt would be okay. I checked the self-inflating mechanism.

We put in at the public access to Sag and started paddling north, but instead of taking the portage to Sag, we stumbled over the rocky rapids and took the Saganaga Corridor instead. Jim had been here two winters ago on a snow machine, and he wanted to see the Corridor in the fall.

I was still bothered by the behavior of Walt and the others, but especially Walt. I remembered Walt's reaching for his knife the night before. Because the Corridor is long and narrow and sheltered on both sides, we had no idea what the lake would be like, but we all made the unspoken assumption that it would be a typical Saganaga day: windy! Even Jim, who had no personal Sag experience, had heard of the lake and its winds and waves. As we approached Clark Island from the south we realized we had all underestimated the lake. It was quite a sight! Whitecaps out on the lake's center became powerful rollers and then fearsome breakers as the waves crashed into the shore of Clark Island and Campers Island farther north. It would be a good four-mile paddle into a very strong northwest wind to American

Point, and even Munker Island, conveniently located in the middle of Sag, wouldn't offer much in the way of a break until we got to its wind shadow.

There were no other canoes to be seen on this blustery, late September day. I could tell that Matt wanted to wait for the wind to die down, but the wind on Sag almost never dies down, and if we waited for pleasant conditions, we might be waiting for a week or more. For ideal conditions, we might have to put the trip off and wait until next summer. That would not do. I told Walt to make the turn west and start pulling to Munker Island. Walt muttered something but made the turn while Dick paddled in the bow. Mark, steering the second canoe with Jim in the bow, also turned towards Munker, but he glared at me as he turned. Why was everyone against me? I turned our canoe and followed. Matt objected but I didn't care.

Walt's canoe was on the left, Mark's was in the middle and ours was on the right. We were positioned line abreast, so they could see what Matt and I, or what I, was doing. I wanted to be last in a single file line, but that was out of my hands now. Paddling in the stern, I managed to keep our canoe angled into the waves that were beating against the bow, but there were many times when I'd overcompensate and take the waves pretty much head on. Matt was getting soaked with cold water and starting to get sick. He was not enjoying himself. Too bad!

We made the two-mile pull to Munker Island's lee and paddled to shore to rest. Matt was wet with spray and shivering, and he wanted to make camp right there. For once, Walt sided with me and shot down that idea. Walt yelled to Matt that we could be here for a full week if we waited for a nice day and that we had to keep moving. By the tone in his voice I could tell that Walt still had last night's argument on his mind. I told Matt that I'd be careful, and I reminded him that I had checked his life vest earlier. I told him that, as a precaution, I'd check it again, but before I could, Walt grabbed it, looked at the self-inflation mechanism, made no adjustments and threw it back at Matt, gruffly saying that it was okay. After resting and doing a map check, we started out for American Point, a full one and one-half miles away.

While we had been resting on the lee shore of Munker Island the wind began to shift to the north, and when Walt and Dick were ready to push off, they could see that the waves had shifted around as well. As soon as they left the lee they were immediately broadsided by the large rollers with whitecaps higher than their gunnels. Mark and Jim also saw what was awaiting them, and they, too, immediately found themselves in the same trouble. Both canoes turned to the northwest to angle into the waves. Matt kept complaining that he didn't want to go, and I indulged him by waiting—waiting until the other canoes were out of earshot, and then some. Then I started across.

Normally I would have cut into the waves just as Walt and Mark were doing, but Matt was now yelling at me to go straight—a straight course, as far as he could see, was the quickest course. Slowly but surely Matt and I went straight, and as we rocked from side to side wallowing in the troughs, I knew what was going to happen. Walt and Mark continued to paddle towards the northwest. We pulled farther and farther apart from them until it finally happened. A large wave rolled Matt and me and almost capsized us to port. Matt and I both leaned over to starboard to compensate, but I leaned way too far, the canoe tipped, and we were thrown into the chilly water. The canoe righted itself. My life preserver, identical to Matt's in that it had a self-inflating mechanism, immediately inflated, but Matt's did not. Matt started to flounder. He thrashed with his arms in panic. Matt called out for Walt and Mark, but I knew that they were too far away to hear him.

All Matt had to do was hold on to the canoe and wait until Walt and Mark made their turns to the southwest, and then they'd probably see us. But Matt was cold and shivering, and he had trouble holding on to the canoe. Eventually both canoes made the cut and started heading southwest. After awhile both canoes adjusted their track and headed directly towards us, as they had obviously seen us in the water. When they got to our canoe I was still holding on, my life preserver keeping me afloat, as I knew it would. But Matt had let go of our canoe out of panic and exhaustion, and he lay floating face down about one hundred yards away. He was easy to spot in his uninflated life preserver. I didn't have to look twice to know that he had drowned.

Mark and Jim paddled to Matt's body, tied a line to it and paddled around Rocky Point, which is the extreme tip of American Point. There were three campsites on American Point, and they towed Matt's body to the first one, where they untied it and dragged it on to shore. In the meantime Walt and Dick had tied a line to my canoe and our gear that had fallen out and towed everything to the same campsite. I swam behind Walt's canoe until I made it to the campsite.

This trip had bad vibes from the very beginning. Communication had been strained, Walt had been arguing, everyone had been cold and distant to me, and now, the trip had claimed Matt.

By now it was late in the day, and we had no choice but to set up camp. Walt and Dick pitched their tent on a large tent pad about fifty feet from the fire grate, and Mark and Jim did the same on a different tent pad. I set up my tent on a wide spot on the trail leading to the latrine. We covered Matt's body with a tarp and then sat down to decide what to do next.

No one said much, probably because there really was nothing to say, but then Jim spoke up. Jim stated the obvious: it was too late in the day to try to paddle out, but he was adamant that we'd have to leave first thing in the morning. But Jim was someone without any Sag Lake experience, and he didn't yet realize that, what with us camped on American Point, we weren't going anyplace soon until the north wind quit blowing. And, as the day had worn on, the wind continued to blow and shift until at seven o'clock it was blowing out of the northeast and even stronger. To get back to where we had started, back to civilization and law enforcement authorities, we'd have to confront a big wind that had already capsized one of our boats and killed one of our party. No one was too excited to try what Jim was insisting we attempt. There was talk of paddling to the southwest and into Cache Bay to contact the Canadian authorities until we realized that, it being late in September, the ranger station was already closed for the season. We explained to Jim that we weren't leaving until the wind died down, but Jim wouldn't hear of it. As far as Jim was concerned, we, and if not we, then he alone, were going out tomorrow. Period.

We had dinner, said a few words about Matt, and then went to bed. It was about nine thirty when I fell asleep.

* * * * *

"Where's Jim?" was the first thing I heard the following morning when I awoke. It was Mark that was yelling.

I crawled out of my tent and met Mark, Walt and Dick at the fire grate. It was seven thirty in the morning. Mark explained that Jim had gotten up to pee at about four thirty. Mark said that he knew the time because he woke up when Jim was putting on his shoes, and he had looked at his watch. But Mark then said that he fell back asleep and didn't realize that Jim hadn't returned. When Mark awoke at six thirty he noticed that Jim wasn't in his sleeping bag, but he thought that Jim was outside someplace. It was not until about twenty minutes ago when Mark got dressed, got out of the tent, looked around the campsite and didn't see him that he realized that Jim was missing. Mark checked and saw our three canoes pulled up on shore, so we at least knew that Jim hadn't tried to go out on his own.

"Well, maybe he walked to the shitter, did you ever think of that?" asked Walt snidely.

"I thought about that," said Mark, "until I saw his pants still in our tent. It's only forty-five degrees, and he wouldn't go to the shitter without his pants if it's only forty-five."

"You've got a good point, Mark," said Dick, but as he said so, Dick was looking at me. Looking at me with an accusing eye, I thought. Dick told the others he thought he had seen me out at about five o'clock. I told everyone that, although I was the last one to go to bed, I did not get out of the tent after that. I showed them my full pee bottle as proof that I hadn't left my tent.

So, we now had a missing trip mate in addition to a dead one. We decided to form a four-abreast search line and walk through the woods. We thought that this would certainly work—our campsite was on the tip of a small peninsula, and a person could not walk very far without seeing water on one side or the other. Once a person saw water, they'd have no trouble at all getting back to the campsite. If they wanted to. And if they were able to.

We walked four abreast, with me on the right, Walt on the left, and Mark and Dick in the middle, keeping sight of one another, until all four of us got to the narrow part of the peninsula. At that point we were convinced that we could not have missed Jim and that he must have continued on, past the narrow neck of the peninsula and deeper into the brush. We decided to continue on as we had, with me on one side, with Walt on the other side, and with Mark and Dick again in the middle. We started walking again, slowly spreading out as the terrain expanded. We kept in sight of each other at first, but the deeper we went into the woods, the more separated we all became. I dropped back a bit to make sure that I didn't miss anything. We had agreed to walk for fifteen minutes, and then Mark and Dick would stop, while Walt and I would turn inward to meet them, the idea being that all four of us would meet in the same place in the middle. After fifteen minutes I turned and started walking toward the middle. Walt must have turned at about the same time because he and I met up with Mark at about the same spot.

But where was Dick?

* * * * *

Mark explained that he and Dick had started out only twenty feet apart, with Dick closer to Walt than me, but the farther they walked, the more separated they had become. Mark explained that he could see that Walt had been walking slowly and that Walt seemed to be hanging back on purpose. Hanging back on purpose? That was suspicious. Walt angrily said that he had been moving slowly so he would not miss anything. Mark had lost sight of Dick early on when Dick had to go around a large tangle of willow. He thought that Dick would come out at the other end, but he didn't.

By now it was past noon and the clouds were gathering for what looked like a storm. We decided to walk back to the peninsula's narrows three abreast in the hope of finding Dick. We started back, this time being very careful to keep each other in sight, walking carefully so we wouldn't miss anything. The three of us got back to the peninsula's narrow neck at about the same time and that's when we saw Dick, standing by a tree.

Jim might very well be lost, but there was no doubt about Dick. Dick was right in front of us, leaning against a birch tree, his eyes half-open, his tongue poking out of his mouth, with his full-size KA-BAR stuck in his neck up to its hilt. He was quite dead.

* * * * *

No one said a word.

The three of us looked at each other.

We returned to the campsite, again walking three abreast, not because we were still looking for Jim, but because two of the three of us could no longer trust the other two. Talk about a Mexican standoff. No one wanted either of the other two behind him.

When we got to the campsite, Mark had to go to the bathroom but quickly realized that Walt and I would not let him out of our sight. For that matter, Walt and I would not remain alone with each other. So, when Mark went to the latrine, he had company, and he took his dump in public, so to speak, and with an audience. He was even too afraid to turn around while he wiped himself.

When we returned, again walking three abreast from the latrine, I realized that I was out of water. I was accompanied, or should I say escorted, by Mark and Walt down to the water's edge, where I filtered water into my water bottle. On the way back, walking along the shore, we found Jim's body—his head had been bashed in like a pumpkin. A large rock with pink curds on it lay close by. The pink curds were Jim's brains.

* * * * *

The three of us sat around the campfire, burning what little firewood that we had left over from last night. It was dark—too dark to get more wood. The tools that we used the day before, an ax for chopping and splitting and a knife for fine splitting, were leaning against the fire grate, ready to be used for getting wood—or for attack or self-defense. No one was about to go off and try to find more wood, as two of the three of us had come to realize that our only hope lay in togetherness. As impossible as that seemed, it was all too true. Without saying anything it was apparent to two of us that only if we stayed together could two of us overpower the one. And the identity of the one that would have to be overpowered was unknown. Unknown except to him.

The gathering storm had finally arrived, and it began to rain. We had three tents pitched and ready to be occupied. Inside each tent were dry clothes and snacks. And, in all likelihood, death for the person seeking comfort and for the person left at the fire grate. The three of us stayed outside, sitting across from each other, staring over a burned out fire, all the while being pelted with cold rain and getting wetter by the moment. There was a flash of lightning followed immediately by a tremendous thunderclap. Startled by the blinding flash of light and the deafening noise, the three of us scattered in three different directions.

Now, things were worse. There was a cold-hearted killer loose on the peninsula, possibly armed and certainly cunning. The two innocents, not knowing which of the other two to trust, could trust neither. The killer, too, had his own worries, for he realized that he could be taken down by the other two. I tried to stay put in my own hiding place for the remainder of the night, waiting for nature's natural dawn to give us the light that we would need to figure things out. But one of us was on the move.

As the small hours of the morning wore on and the campsite ever so slightly started to lighten, through the heavy, foggy, weeping mist, there appeared, hanging from a large tree, the body of a camper, twisting slowly in the wind. A rope was tied around his neck, and his feet dangled ten feet above the ground. His head was bent at an odd angle, and the seat of his pants were soiled.

It was then that Walt and I looked at each other from opposite ends of the campsite clearing. It was at that very moment that both of us, at the exact same moment, finally realized just who the killer was.

The ax and knife were still close by the fire grate—either could be used as a weapon for attack or as a weapon for self-defense. Walt and I dashed for the fire grate at the same time.

All that remained to be decided was whether the killer would be killed.

Or, maybe there were two killers....

ON GOING SOLO

It's happened to all of us, and if it hasn't happened to you yet, it's going to happen, sooner or later. Maybe even tomorrow.

Your loyal bowman—the same guy that has been in the front of your canoe for the last dozen trips—just called. He twisted his ankle last night. Or his daughter twisted her ankle last night. Or his daughter's soccer team advanced to the league championship last night. Whatever the reason, he has to pull out of Thursday's canoe trip to Basswood Lake. Or maybe your best friend from college, who was one of your bridesmaids at your wedding and who has been your hiking partner since even before then, had a death in her family, and she just called to tell you that she can't do that backpacking trip to Isle Royale on Friday. Or maybe you've been thinking that it's time to tell your canoeing partner or your hiking partner that this time you want to try something different.

Regardless of how it comes about, sooner or later you're going to be presented with the opportunity to travel alone.

Most people review their options and consider all the reasons why they should, or why they shouldn't, make the attempt to travel solo.

Under the "should" column is the romantic notion of a solitary person facing the wilderness on their own terms, while being presented by Mother Nature with the perfect weather and perfect scenery to accommodate their vision and complete the picture. In your mind's eye you can see it oh so clearly—an idyllic image, frozen in time. You, the way you want to be, in the wilderness.

But if you are an experienced visitor to the outdoors, the Voice of Experience (i.e., reality) sooner or later barges into your daydream and splashes some cold water on your face and forces you to think things through. Perhaps the discussion between reality and your ego goes something like this:

Reality: "So, you're thinking about a solo canoe trip, are you?"

Ego: "Yeah, it'll be great!"

Reality: "You understand that whatever gear you'll need, you'll have to carry by yourself?"

Ego: "Not a problem—I've carried lots of gear before."

Reality: "No, no, no, you didn't hear me. I didn't say that you'd have to carry lots of gear. What I said was that you'd have to carry *all* the gear."

Ego: "I can do it."

Reality: "Everything you'll need you'll have to carry."

Ego: "Understood."

Reality: "And you can't carry it if you don't remember it in the first place."

Ego: "Not a problem."

Reality: "This is important, so I'm going to say it again. Every little thing you'll need, you're going to have to carry. And you're going to be responsible for remembering to bring it in the first place. Do you understand that?"

Ego: "I've got lots of camping trips behind me. I know what I'm doing."

Reality: "You're pretty weak on your knots. Tom usually sets up the tarp and ties the knots."

Ego: "I'm not leaving until the day after tomorrow. I've got time to learn those knots."

Reality: "As I recall, you like to sit around a campfire at night. Who's going to get the firewood?"

Ego: "I'll get the firewood."

Reality: "Are you going to carry the saw and hatchet?"

Ego: (pausing slightly) "Tom usually does that, but I guess I'll have to."

Reality: "Are you going to want to cover the seating area around the fire grate in case it rains?"

Ego: "Of course."

Reality: "Well, you're going to need the tarp and the pole."

Ego: "I'll fit them in my pack."

Reality: "And poly cord. You'll need lots of poly cord."

Ego: "I've got it. And I've watched Tom set up the tarp. It doesn't look so hard."

Reality: "You'll have to bring a water filter, you know."

Ego: (proudly) "I've already got one."

Reality: "But can you clean the filter when it clogs? Have you forgotten what happened two years ago on the Perent River trip?"

Ego: "I'll carry an extra filter."

Reality: "You'll need a stove. And fuel. And extra fuel."

Ego: "I've already got…"

Reality: "And matches."

Ego: (boasting) "I've got a lighter."

Reality: "Not good enough. Sometimes lighters don't work. You need a backup. You need a lighter *and* matches."

Ego: "I suppose it wouldn't hurt, but…"

Reality: "Sometimes stoves simply quit. And sometimes they won't start in the first place. Are you ready to do all of your cooking over the fire grate like you and Tom had to do for those three nights on Little Gabbro in 2006?"

Ego: "I can…"

Reality: (interrupting) "And a cook kit. You can't forget the cook kit. Are you going to carry one or two pots along with the frying pan?"

Ego: (hesitating) "Maybe I can get by with only one pot."

Reality: "You'll be out four days and three nights. That means four breakfasts, four lunches and four dinners."

Ego: "I can…"

Reality: "Are you going to dehydrate your food to save weight?"

Ego: "I'll have to start doing that…"

Reality: (interrupting again) "And don't forget your snacks."

Ego: "Right. Snacks."

Reality: "You'll have to pack the tent, your sleeping pad, your sleeping bag, clothes, extra clothes, rain gear…"

Ego: (interrupting) "I checked the forecast. It's not supposed to rain."

Reality: "Better to have it and not need it than to need it and not have it. You *will* be packing your rain gear!"

Ego: "Yeah, I suppose I should. Well, my rain jacket anyway."

Reality: "Your rain jacket *and* your rain pants!"

Ego: (annoyed) "OK, OK, OK."

Reality: "Water bottle, bug dope, nylon cord, sunscreen, map, compass, flashlight, batteries, extra batteries, extra flashlight, toilet paper, gloves, first aid kit, sewing kit, repair kit, stove repair kit, mattress repair kit, fire starter, notebook and pencil, knife, Leatherman tool, pack cover, knife, plastic bags, toothbrush and toothpaste, extra pair of glasses, sunglasses, knife, water boots, camp shoes, soap, a pack to carry everything in, a second pack to carry some of the gear because putting it all in one pack will be too heavy..."

Ego: (interrupting) "Most of that stuff I've..."

Reality: "Canoe, paddle, extra paddle, life preserver, portage yoke, permit, painters..."

Ego: (interrupting) "Are you trying to talk me out of not doing a solo trip?"

Reality: "And a knife. Have I already mentioned a knife?"

Ego: (slightly depressed) "Yeah, this is the fourth time you've mentioned a knife."

Reality: "And it goes without saying, or maybe it should be said, that along with all of that gear comes the responsibility to properly *use* that gear: the safe way to use a saw and a hatchet, the proper way to rig a tarp, the easiest way to build a fire, the quickest way to build a *survival* fire, how to get a stubborn stove to light, the best place to pitch your tent, reading the weather, reading a map, using a compass, knowing basic first aid, because simply having the first aid kit along really isn't enough, knowing how to make emergency repairs to a piece of critical equipment or clothing in the field, being able to handle a solo canoe in calm water, loading, unloading, getting in, getting out, and then handling the canoe when the winds pick up and the waves are licking the gunnels..."

Ego: (irritated) "Who do you think you are, anyway?"

Reality: "Me? I'm reality, otherwise known as the Voice of Experience. You've met me many times. Every time you've forgotten something on a trip, every time you've done something wrong on a trip, every time you could have done something better on a trip. That's when we've met. You and I know each other so well that we're on a first name basis. That's who I am and that's who you're talking to."

Ego: "Well…"

Reality: "Everything that you'll need and everything that has to get done is going to be *your* responsibility."

Ego: (not very convincingly) "Yeah, I know. But it'll all be worth it—being able to sit back and relax, sit back and take it all in. No pressure, no worries, no nothing.

Reality: "You haven't heard a word that I've said, have you? You're going to be doing everything that has to be done. You're not going to have any spare time."

Ego: (deflated) "Maybe I should just reschedule the trip so that Tom can make it."

Reality: "Oh, I forgot. You'll have to do the dishes too!"

Many people initially think that they would like to try a solo trip, but by the time they consider everything that is involved, they pass on the opportunity. The simple truth is that most people, when presented with the chance to travel solo, find a reason not to. And in finding a reason not to, they very rarely admit to their friends and partners the *real* reason why they don't travel alone. They almost always fail to admit it to themselves either, at least not consciously, although the reason is always there, staring them right in the face.

It's that big elephant in the room that we can no longer ignore.

It's the *psychological* component of travelling solo.

A very experienced wilderness traveler recently confided in me that, although he feels comfortable enough on a solo day hike or solo day ski, he just doesn't have the emotional makeup for an overnight solo trip. I have the necessary emotional makeup, but only just barely, and only by the slimmest of margins. The fragile nature of *my* emotional makeup when a solo trip is in the works becomes readily apparent when I realize that, although I'll plan and pack for a four day/three night trip, I'll invariably come in off the trail early, with extra food and extra supplies in my pack. I've come in early many times. For that matter, my emotional makeup limits me to overnight solo summer trips if I'll be on the water, and to late spring or early fall trips if I'll be on foot. But then I have a winter camping partner that once crossed the Quetico—alone—in the winter.

This isn't meant to be a commentary on the relative sangfroid of my friends and me, but it is important to realize that, if you are going to do a solo trip, being able to manage your gear is really not as important as being able to manage yourself. And it's that thought—"I'm going to be all alone and without anybody to talk to or help out in case things get dicey"—that prompts most people to find other things to do.

So why bother? What's the point in attempting a solo trip if there's a chance you're not going to come back alive, and even if you do, you'll be working harder than you want to, without anyone to talk to? Seriously, why travel alone?

For starters, there's that romantic notion that it's you and the wilderness and nothing else. You are living life on *your* terms. The importance of this notion *cannot* be overstated. There is much to be said for being in total control—going where you want to go, when you want to go, how you want to go, starting and stopping as you like, seeing what you want to see and doing what you want to do. In a word, freedom. You even get to pick dinnertime. You may even decide not to do the dishes. No one will care. For people that have a dog, Fido or Spot or Rover can provide tremendous emotional support. You'll still be responsible for the camp chores, but your dog will lick the dishes clean. They make great listeners, too.

Travelling solo gives you the opportunity to learn. Many educators will tell you that they really didn't start to truly understand their specialty until they started to teach it to others. Travelling solo forces you to teach yourself to do things better, to do things the right way.

Travelling solo also gives you the opportunity to learn something more about this child that your parents raised. You have a chance to learn something more about this person that your spouse or partner shares their life with. You will learn some things that make you feel uncomfortable, perhaps even ashamed. But you'll also learn that you can live in the wilderness on your own and without help.

"But I'm too old to do a solo trip," comes the protest. Nonsense! It's true that from a *physical* point of view your average twenty-year-old will fare better than your average sixty-year-old will. Yet there is much to be found in the phrase "not the boldest, but the oldest." The older you are, the better you can handle a solo trip from a psychological point of view. Remember, it's not about managing your gear—it's about managing yourself.

"But I don't have the experience to do a solo trip." That's why you start slowly, and with small steps. You can learn more on your first solo trip than you'll learn in your next ten trips. You learn very quickly, and if you're careful, you're not going to get into trouble.

When you come off the trail after a solo trip and rejoin civilization you'll find yourself dealing with people that are spooked by their own shadow, people that live their lives by a horoscope, and people that have to rely on gravity to help them find the floor when they roll out of bed in the morning. And there you are, tired and beat up and smelly, with bumps and bruises on your shins after communing with Nature by relying on your wits, your experience and whatever you carried on your back. It's not even a fair fight anymore.

Solo tripping may not be for everyone, but everyone should try it at least once.

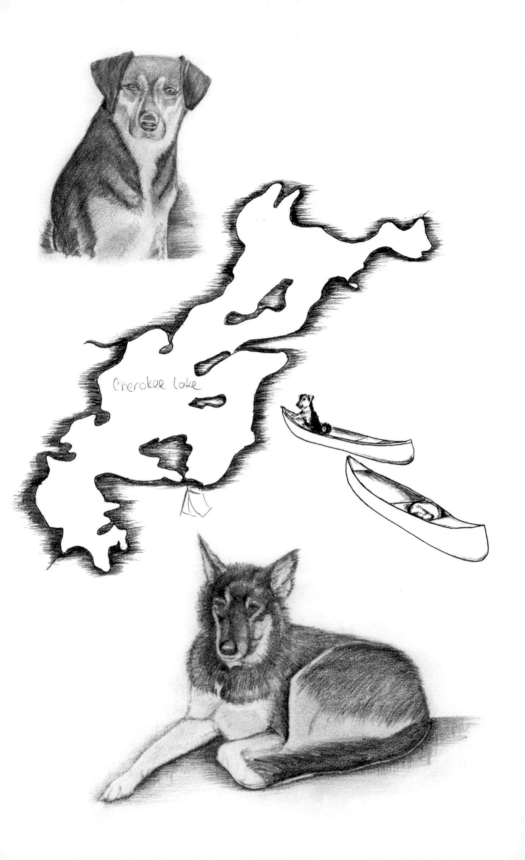

Cherokee Lake

CANOE CAMPING: IT'S NOT JUST FOR PEOPLE ANYMORE

Love the animals. God has given them the rudiments of thought and joy untroubled. Don't trouble them, don't harass them, don't deprive them of their happiness, don't work against God's intent.
—Dostoevsky, *The Brothers Karamazov*

Willow is one of my all-time favorite dogs. She is part something and part something else and I don't really care. Her facial markings are perfectly symmetrical, as if an artist drew one-half of her face and then ran the drawing through a reverse-image copier. Her colors are black, brown, tan and white. She has a wet nose. She also has an enormous voice for her small size. I think she's four or five years old, and she is powerfully built. Her triangle ears flop down on either side of her face.

Willow lives in the middle of Wisconsin, but there are times when I wished that she lived with me. My bride of twenty-five years, who is allergic to animal dander, could live in our heated garage where she would be most comfortable, and Willow could stay in the house with me. The garage already has running water, and a portable commode could be easily installed.

Willow is a rescue, and I'm glad that her masters saved her. I used Willow as a model for a dog in a different story, but in that story I named her Smiles. Willow is very affectionate, and although she likes to lay in the hammock with her male master and give him kisses, she has told me in strictest confidence that I am a better kisser than her male master is.

I see Willow at least several days once a year, sometimes for several days twice a year, but never enough.

Willow has an older brother, Ranger. Ranger is also a rescue. Whereas Willow is gregarious and outgoing, Ranger is more reserved, to the point of being aloof. Ranger is taller and thinner than Willow, and he is quite handsome. He is black and brown too, but he has less tan and more white than Willow. He rarely barks. Maybe because he is older, or maybe because he feels the need to set an example for his little sister, Ranger acts more dignified than Willow, although he still wallows in the dry, dusty, dirt. He has been known to stare at a tree for longer than he should, waiting for the campsite chipmunk to come down, but he's wasting his time because he could never catch the chipmunk anyway.

Although both dogs are well behaved, on one particular morning at the campsite at the southeast corner of Cherokee Lake when I was not looking, Ranger entered the prohibited kitchen area and lapped up my powdered egg mix to which I had just added water. Ranger's female master scolded him severely for doing so, but I saw that she was laughing while she was doing it, laughing at me because I no longer had a breakfast to eat. When I caught Ranger with his muzzle in my bowl, I scolded him too. He looked back at me, as if to say, "Well, what did you expect? I'm only a dog, ya know!!"

If Ranger were human, he'd have a lot of girlfriends because of his looks. If Willow were human, she'd have a lot of boyfriends because she would be unable to say, "No."

Both Willow and Ranger have been on the last several annual canoe trips. They love to chase each other up and down the portages, constantly getting in the way of cranky people carrying awkward canoes on their shoulders who are desperately looking for solid footing but who have to be careful not to step on the dogs. When they are in the canoe on the water, Willow sits in the bow between the legs of her female master. She sits up so that she can see what is going on. Ranger lies between his male master's legs in the stern. He doesn't really care what is going on. They both wear dog floatation devices that their masters bought for them. The dog floatation devices have pockets on them so that the dogs can carry their own food, treats and toys, but on one annual canoe trip their male master had each of them carry a plastic bottle of beer for him to drink at the campsite. Judging from the little stickers that both have worn on their collars, both dogs vote straight Republican.

I am writing this about two weeks before our annual Boundary Waters canoe trip with the dogs' masters. This year's canoe trip will be our seventh trip with them. It is a wonderful tradition that we have going, and I look forward to the day, a few years from now, when I will be talking to a total stranger that I've met on a portage, and I will tell this total stranger that the guy coming up the trail with the dog under his feet and the Minnesota II on his shoulders will, with me, be celebrating our tenth annual Boundary Waters canoe trip that very evening. That night we will enjoy warm beer, but Willow and Ranger, being dogs, will know better than to have any.

Both of their masters treat their dogs well, and for their part, both Willow and Ranger would, without hesitation, lay down their lives for Dan and Mary.

These are the two canine personalities that will be participating in the upcoming annual canoe trip. And I am their Uncle Steve. I am an uncle to all furry animals.

If prior trips are a guide, I would expect this year's trip to go something like this:

Willow and Ranger's masters have already been talking to them about the upcoming canoe trip. Dogs apparently don't understand a single word of the King's English, but they understand baby dog talk fluently, which is why all dog owners talk that way. By now Willow and Ranger have been told that they will be driving to Duluth to see Uncle Steve and other less interesting smelling humans from Duluth, Southern Wisconsin and a funny foreign country called California. Willow and Ranger are the last things to get packed and then the family sets off, destination Duluth, in their big, blue hrududu.*

When Willow and Ranger arrive in Duluth and are let out of the big, blue hrududu, they go about their business, Ranger looking for a tree and Willow looking for a flat surface. The dogs are fed and

---

Hrududu is rabbitspeak for "motor vehicle," per *Watership Down*, an extraordinary 1972 novel by Richard Adams, which if you have not read is to your profound loss.

watered and put down for the night, while the adults catch up on things and put a serious dent in my beer locker. The following day is a travel day, preceded by an evening of repacking and re-repacking until everyone goes to bed.

During the following morning, while the adults will be looking forward to getting on the water, getting camp set up and relaxing, both Willow and Ranger will be busy exercising their sniffers, constantly searching out new smells and odors in the parking lot. Each odor will be analyzed, first going through the dog's digital food/not food sensor. A dog's digital food/not food sensor consists of highly refined, specially adapted nerve endings in the dog's nose that instantly inform the dog's brain if this particular lead is worth pursuing (eat it or keep looking).

If the odor is suggestive of a nutrition source, the source will be tracked down and consumed, with identification coming later. If the odor comes back as "not food," it will then be run through the dog's database of non-food items in an attempt to determine if it can still be eaten. A piece of rotting wood is an example of something that is not food but which can still be eaten. Willow and Ranger have learned that there are many things that are not food that can still be eaten.

New plants, new animals, new insects all go through a dog's digital food/not food sensor. If the dog decides that the odor is not suggestive of a food source and that, whatever it is, it should not be eaten, chances are the dog will still eat it anyway and worry about the consequences later. I have watched dogs vomit up prior swallowings, and I am convinced that dog vomit and the process of dog vomiting are not as bad as people vomit and the process of people vomiting.

Dogs have other talents that humans can only stare at in disbelief. It is not uncommon for a wheel dog pulling a dogsled to lick with enjoyment the anus of the dog ahead of it, but should the dog ahead of it actually drop a stool on the trail, the wheel dog will jump over it or jump off to the side so as to not get its paws dirty with something that it is more than willing to put in its mouth.

It's things like these that, when it comes time to get affectionate with a canine, separate the real dog lovers like Willow and Ranger's masters and me from all the rest.

By the time the adults have got packs in the canoes and the canoes in the water, it's time to get Willow and Ranger. By now they have had about thirty minutes to explore their new surroundings. Their masters know without seeing that each has eaten something that will be coming up again, the only question being whether what comes up again will come up while Willow and Ranger are on a portage (preferred) or while Willow and Ranger are still in the canoe (not preferred). A short while later we are on the water, and even though I am thirty feet to their starboard, I hear Ranger's male master scolding Ranger, and I know that whatever it is that Ranger ate earlier, it is presently in the bottom of their canoe, with some of it probably on Ranger's male master's shin and foot. I chuckle to myself accordingly.

Normally we paddle in, set up a base camp, and do day trips from there. Five portages from start to finish mean that Willow and Ranger will have five opportunities to trip up people on the portages, be they part of our group or total strangers, the dogs being nondiscriminating. To warn friends and strangers of their impending approach, Willow and Ranger's masters have affixed little bells to their collars. When I hear the bells approaching I freeze and bend both legs, naively hoping that I will be better able to absorb Willow's blow than if I have straight, rigid legs. I don't worry about Ranger; Ranger is too much of an older sibling to do anything to make him look foolish in the eyes of his little sister. Besides, Ranger has a nice, graceful lope that he is always in control of. Willow, on the other hand, is best described as a fire hydrant on legs (she's about that size) barreling down the portage, and given her mass and the velocity at which she moves, if she brushes against me, I am going down, canoe and all, regardless of if I have taken the precaution of bending my knees or not.

Both Willow and Ranger insist on bathing at the beginning and end of each portage, which gives me further reason to chuckle, as they climb back into the canoe, getting their masters wet in the process.

But after a fashion we arrive at a campsite, set up camp, and start relaxing. Almost immediately Ranger is sitting back on his haunches, head uplifted, eyes focused on the campsite chipmunk that is taunting Ranger from high up in the tree that Ranger cannot even begin to figure out how to climb. Willow, on the other hand, is busy snapping at dragonflies, although sometimes she appears to be snapping at nothing at all, and I find myself wondering if she is hallucinating, possibly having an adverse reaction to the rotten piece of wood that she ate two portages ago, the remnants of which are still stuck to her female master's foot.

So goes the week in the woods, with most of the humans enjoying themselves, like Ranger, by doing nothing, and Willow enjoying herself, like me, by doing everything. To suggest that Ranger's sole interest at the campsite is the campsite chipmunk would not be an overstatement. On the third evening of the annual canoe trip a few years' back, we were visited by a pair of loons that stopped by to serenade us. Willow was so excited that she began to hyperventilate. Ranger was so excited that he fell asleep.

The high point of Willow's and Ranger's day is food time, which usually coincides with human dinnertime, although as the dogs' Uncle Steve I have been known to sneak them various treats at any time. Both dogs have trained their female master well. When they both sit back on their haunches and look at their female master, the latter is compelled to get their respective bowls and fill them with some boring dog food that is not as enticing as what the humans are then preparing. Both dogs will then stare at their master and telepathically encourage her to say the magic word. Once their female master says the magic word, the dogs inhale their dinner and then come hanging around the prohibited kitchen area looking for handouts, the receipt of which is dependent on how closely their masters are watching. I have learned that Ranger can be bribed with peanut butter.

If a human is lucky he or she will hear a wolf howl in the night. If a human is especially lucky, it will happen when he or she has a dog in camp, and the human has the opportunity to watch how their tame house pet reacts. The howling wolf is talking to its own kind, but the dog acts like an eavesdropper, which is what it is. A house dog that hears a wild wolf is a perfect example of the classic nurture versus nature debate, but at a canine level. How much of us, as humans, or as dogs, is attributable to how we were raised, and how much of us is attributable to who we were born to be? Dogs are only very recently domesticated, and they are not far removed from that truly wild voice howling in the distance. Would domesticated dogs that hear their distant cousin howl in the night give up the comforts of living with humans for the experience of living their true selves? Dog owners, take note: Although this is your vacation, your chance to get away from it all, it is an opportunity for your dog to ever so slightly experience what it really is—a wild animal. Let your dog do so. Let your dog relish the experience. Watch closely as your dog experiences the wilderness. Your domesticated house pet is closer to the wilderness than you will ever be. Appreciate your dog enjoying its essence.

When it's time to tear down the camp and paddle back to the real world, the humans are depressed, but to Willow and Ranger, it's just another day. Animals, unlike humans, live in the present and don't concern themselves with what happened yesterday. They cannot even grasp the concept of a tomorrow. As a result, animals are happier than their humans. The trip out is just another set of chances for Willow and Ranger to race the length of the portages while getting underfoot of humans who don't want anything under their feet.

When the trip is over the humans go back to their daily lives and think about the fine time they all had. But I suspect that for Willow and Ranger, returning from a canoe trip in the wilderness, it's different. I suspect that for several days Willow and Ranger are both a bit more wild than they were before the trip. Of course, Willow and Ranger cannot realize this. But for several days afterwards Willow and Ranger are both a little more like wild wolves than before they left.

And that's why dogs should go on canoe trips.

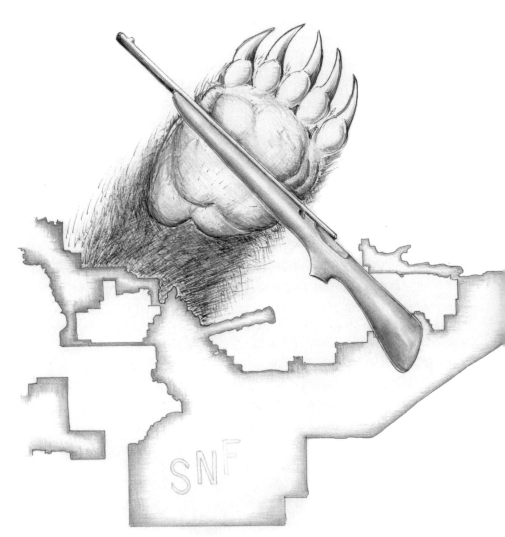

Superior National Forest

THE CONTEST

Holding on to anger is like grasping a hot coal with the intent of throwing it at someone else; you are the one who gets burned.
—Siddhartha Gautama

The date for this match between the two heavyweights had been scheduled by the fates for the second day of the third week of September, although neither of the match's antagonists knew it yet. Given that the issue between the combatants had been festering for well over a decade, one might have anticipated more of a buildup than what would be witnessed. But there would be no buildup at all. No publicity was to be given to the event, and tickets would not be sold to the curious. The location of the bout could vaguely be described as the Superior National Forest. Even the time of the encounter had been unspecified; the battle would commence when the warriors met, and the time of their meeting would be dependent on their skill, cunning, ingenuity and pure blind luck. The victor would not be recognized by any audience as the champion after vanquishing his foe. For this was not to be a Sunday afternoon competition between two opposing players or teams for a trophy. The bout would not be professionally programmed and presented as entertainment for the hero-worshiping fans of the players. This was to be nothing other than a contest between old foes, each with a score to settle with the other. A grudge match, pure and simple, with the winner being awarded another day to live and the loser being visited by a violent demise. Both contestants, in the separate and distinct manner of their own kind, frequently thought about meeting the other since their first encounter so long ago. And both, again in the separate and distinct manner of their own kind, remembered how that encounter had ended: with permanent injuries to both. And in a few weeks' time, each would get their chance to close the books on this long outstanding account, in a colorful forest destined to be foggy, cool and wet on the day of reckoning.

It would seem that the contestants were evenly matched; whatever advantages one would have would be cancelled by advantages of a different nature possessed by the other.

The first contestant was eighteen years old and weighed more than five hundred pounds. It measured eighty-four inches long and stood forty-two inches at the shoulder and, even for its kind, was unusually large. It lived mostly on berries, nuts, grasses, carrion and insect larvae. It was amazingly nimble and quick, given its bulk, and it could easily run in excess of thirty miles per hour for short distances, although it was also prone to overheating when it did so. However, overheating would not be a concern, for it could certainly run down its opponent most effortlessly. It had been blessed at birth, as were other members of its kind, with color vision, which was unusual among animals, and both its vision and its hearing were at least as good as its opponent's. Its sense of smell had been modestly described as "excellent" but was more accurately credited as being the most sensitive in the animal kingdom. Typically a loner, it was very intelligent and curious. But, atypically for its kind, it was not shy around its natural enemy, and as it had matured it had developed a tendency to stalk them. It was strong. Very strong. It could easily kill its opponent with a single swipe of its massive front paw. It was black and habitually bad-tempered, for a long-ago injury inflicted by its opponent had never healed and kept it in constant pain. Ursus americanus was its species. It was a black bear.

The second contestant was forty-two years of age, stood seventy-six inches tall and weighed two hundred and thirty pounds. It, too, was large for its kind, although certainly no match for its opponent. When compared with its opponent it was slower and weaker and had a pathetic sense of smell, although its hearing and eyesight, as corrected, were both adequate. Socially, it was a gregarious creature, prone to displays of pride when recalling its conquests. It was also omnivorous, which explained why, a dozen years ago, it had tried to kill the bear.

Compared with the bear, it would be no match in a physical confrontation but for the facts that it was self-aware and able to reason and its kind possessed the highest and most refined intellect in the forest; plus the fact that when the struggle began it would be armed with a weapon. Its species was Homo sapiens. It was a man.

The high-powered rifle that he always carried while in the forest would give the man a seemingly distinct advantage over the bear, for while the bear would have to fight at close quarters, the man could fight from afar. But the encounter would take place not in a neutral setting, but rather on the bear's home turf—the forest. And although the man was a veteran of the forest, his experiences therein were no match for those of the bear, who was born and raised in the same range that it today called home: a heavily wooded area approximately seventy-five square miles in size. While the man relied on his intellect to assist him with life's many challenges, the bear relied on its finely attuned senses, all of which had become even more refined and honed as the bear aged.

Most of the handicappers of such an event, after considering the strengths and weaknesses of each opponent, would rate it a toss-up, with even money on each, which meant that all bets would be off, although there were some that considered the bear's developing penchant for stalking humans as heavily weighing the odds in the bear's favor. For this was a bear that would not avoid humans but rather would seek them out, much as victims are stalked by a predator, which is what the bear had become.

The contest, although not involving canines or lupines, would most certainly be between two alpha males, both past their physical primes, but both sharpened by the experiences of life, which more than made each a match for the younger and more youthful of their respective species. Two true heavyweights. The man would have the rifle, but the bear would have the unparalleled ferocity of a wild beast, the level of which the man could not even hope to imagine.

While normally a human would judge the success or failure of a bear hunting season by if it shot a bear, the best that an individual bear could do would be to simply hold its own—to not get killed. The best that an ordinary bear could do would be to survive the day. But the stakes for this contest between the two old adversaries were identical for each—the bear's unusual temperament guaranteed that either it would perish or the man would. There would be a clear winner in the joust. One would live, and one would not.

The initial encounter between the two had occurred a dozen years ago, by chance, in the early summer, and when the bear was supposedly protected from human assault, the bear hunting season still being two months away. The bear was six years old at the time, a robust adolescent, when it was spied by the man who was armed with a high-powered rifle. The man had been hunting deer out of season. The man was thirty years old, but he had already developed a disdain for regulations that limited his activities, hence his being in a deer stand on an early July evening, hoping to take a deer that he had noticed frequenting the salt lick that he had set out as bait.

But on this particular evening, instead of attracting a deer, the salt lick had brought in the bear. The man, having earlier climbed down from the deer stand to relieve himself, turned and found himself staring eye-to-eye at a black bear that was already of extraordinary size. At that time the bear did not react but rather continued to observe as the man slowly walked the seventy-five feet back to his deer stand. The bear saw the man climb the tree, pick up a long length of black stick and point it in its general direction. All at once the bear saw the man jerk, felt a sharp pain in its left back paw, and heard a loud "CRACK." The bear, not being a creature of deduction, did not realize that it had been shot by the man and would not have developed its festering compulsion for revenge but for what was yet to come.

The bear, possessed of keenly developed senses but without the ability to reason, was incapable of realizing that it had been harmed by the man. The bear then saw the man hold the long black stick up a second time, and the bear saw the man jerk again. The bear felt a sharp pain in its left shoulder and heard a second loud "CRACK." The bear was now in considerable pain and fell over backwards, and as it did so, it hit its head on a large rock. The bear was dazed and lay still, and to the poaching hunter in the deer stand, it appeared quite dead.

The man, giddy with exaltation, climbed down from the deer stand, almost falling in the process. He walked up to the bear slowly and warily, keeping his rifle at the ready, for he had heard that sometimes big game that appeared to be dead was anything but. The man walked to within a rifle-length of the bear and prodded it, the black muzzle of his rifle burrowing into the black fur of the beast. The man, now convinced that the bear was dead, walked back to the deer stand to retrieve his camera. He wanted to take a picture of himself standing over his conquest. The man set up his tripod, mounted the camera, set the self-timer, pushed the shutter and quickly walked back to the bear and waited for the camera to capture the moment. The man thought that a second picture would be legitimate insurance, so he walked back to the camera, reset the self-timer and hurried back to the bear. This time, for added effect, the man put his right foot on the bear's left shoulder, and the camera captured a look of triumph and superiority on the man's face.

It was then the bear regained consciousness.

Slowly it opened its eyes and surveyed what it could see. It swiveled its ears to better pick up any sounds that might be nearby. But before the bear could begin to process the sights and sounds that its eyes and ears were delivering, it was overcome by the repugnant and repulsive odor of the man who was grinding his foot into its wounded shoulder. The bear was unable to associate the black stick or the loud "CRACK" with the pain that it felt in its rear paw and front shoulder, but the bear immediately and for the rest of its life associated the pain that it felt with the overcoming stench of the man. And it was not just the stench of man that the bear would never forget, but rather the unique stench of this particular man that was standing atop him, with his foot pressing into the bear's wound.

The bear immediately reacted by rolling over, exposing its front right paw and, in the process, knocking the startled man over. The bear took a swipe at the man and hit him. Long, yellow claws ripped through the man's wool shirt, ripped through the man's undershirt and then ripped through the man's skin and arm muscle, shredding it. The man screamed out in pain and tried to roll away, but not fast enough. The bear's second swipe caught the man's face and ripped half of it away. The man screamed again but not as loud this time, his left cheek having been torn by the bear's claws.

The man, grievously wounded and hideously appearing, ran for his life, abandoning the long black stick that the bear still could not appreciate the significance of. For its part, the bear tried to offer chase but immediately stumbled, for it could not put any weight on its left shoulder, and it would be unable to do so for many days.

The first encounter between the man and the bear had ended in a draw. The man ultimately lost none of his mobility, but he never fully recovered the use of his arm, and his face, although the subject of many surgeries, never ever again appeared anything close to normal. The injuries left the man with deep hatred, fueled by revenge, and he made it his life's goal to bring down his attacker.

The bear's appearance suffered not at all from the encounter with the man, but the bear did not have a vain streak and could not have cared less. However, the bear would be forever hobbled by the wound to its shoulder, which would cause it more pain or less pain, depending on the weather, for the rest of its life. The injury to the bear's shoulder also affected its ability to feed, although by relying on its senses the bear was still able to obtain appropriate nourishment, which, combined with its genes, gave the bear unusual size and heft. The bear, being a creature without emotion, nevertheless forever associated the pain in its shoulder with the stench that scarred its nostrils.

Neither the man nor the bear would ever forget the other. The man became driven by revenge. The bear became driven by the unique odor that it forever linked to its wounded shoulder.

The subsequent years saw both the man and the bear rise to the top of their respective hierarchies. For the bear it meant rising to the top of the forest. For the man it meant rising to the top of his business. Each achieved success, and given the power that each wielded, each had the pick of its mate, and over the years the bear and the man had both enjoyed several.

The subsequent years also found the man's employment transferring him to a different location, which interfered with his lust for revenge.

But to the forest he returned when he could, which numbered five times. During all five visits, when he came to the forest, he came alone, for he wanted no distractions, and he wanted no witnesses, his intent being to do what had to be done, and to do it in a most vicious and vengeful manner.

The bear, for its part, stayed within its range, the throbbing in its shoulder a constant reminder of the man who had crippled it. The man knew how to seek out the bear, but the bear never knew when the man was coming. And for that reason, the ultimate showdown between the two was dependent on the man's schedule. When the man came to the forest, he came with one specific goal in mind. The bear never knew when the man was coming, but during each of his five visits the man left his singular, telltale odor, which the bear immediately recognized when it detected it. However, the bear's range was too large, and when the man had been on one side of the bear's range, the bear had been on the other. Each of the man's five return visits ended with frustration for the man, for he knew that the bear was there, somewhere. And after the man left each of the five times, the bear happened across the man's stale odor, but never stale enough to fail to rekindle the memory of years past.

It has been said that God takes care of major events and leaves the minor ones to random chance. So it was that the man planned a sixth vacation back to the Superior National Forest in mid-September, the third week of the month to be exact. As in years past, he swore off companionship and the services of a guide, preferring to work alone, as he knew the bear would. Deliberate planning by the man led to him staking out high ground downwind of a little creek that offered a clear shooting lane at anything that stopped for a drink of water. Deliberate planning by the man led to him baiting the stream with food that he knew bears would find irresistible. But random chance led to a very temporary but significant change in the direction of the wind, a change in wind direction that the man did not immediately notice but which brought to the bear, then two miles distant to the man's left, the unmistakable odor of its hated enemy. The bear was immediately on the move, following the odor that it had first sensed twelve years earlier. The man, watching the creek for any movement, watched unaware of the menace approaching from his left quarter.

The change in wind direction had been temporary but long enough to bring the bear to within visual distance of the man, which the bear observed was still holding a black stick, the significance of which the bear still did not and could not understand. The distance between the two was less than three hundred yards, a distance that the bear could cover in less than twenty seconds if it wanted to. But it didn't want to, just yet.

For the bear had not lived for eighteen years in the wild, nor had it attained its enormous size, by being careless and hurried. The bear instinctively knew that it would be better to take its time and size up its enemy. So the bear waited, watching the man from behind a thicket of alder.

The man, for his part, had not achieved his successes by being unobservant, and after awhile he noticed that the cool breeze that he had felt on the front of his mangled face now massaged his right cheek. Slowly the man turned his head to the left and looked through the light fog that had formed. The man saw nothing out of the ordinary; in fact, all the man saw were trees dripping with rain and, further back, a thicket of alder, thick enough to hide behind. Without hesitation the man released the safety of his rifle.

The bear saw the man, smelled the man. The man sensed the bear to be near. The contest was on.

Both knew that they were in the presence of the other; the bear by sight and smell and the man by mere feeling, for the man had developed instincts of his own. The man held the advantage by virtue of the rifle, but the advantage was nullified by the simple fact that, although the rifle could reach out a considerable distance, the rifle was useless unless its holder has something to aim at. This the man did not have. The bear knew that it could charge the man and reach him quickly, but the bear instinctively knew that such would be a mistake, and indeed it would have been, for the bear would have been an easy target for the man once it emerged from the alder.

Each considered their options in their own distinct way; the man by reasoning the problem and the bear by instinctively feeling the problem. The man decided that he held the high ground and that, because he had a clear fire lane toward the alder, he should remain where he was. The bear, oblivious to the threat posed by the black stick, nevertheless decided to remain where it was. A waiting match began, the bear watching the man and the man feeling the bear.

Patience is an interesting commodity; most humans will admit that they don't have enough when, in point of fact, most humans don't have any at all. But to a disciplined mind, patience can be consciously invoked at will, and the man had a disciplined mind. To a wild beast, patience is a concept that cannot be understood, let alone invoked. Animals are naturally unhurried because animals don't have any sense of time. The man remained patient because he willed himself to remain patient. But the bear decided that it was time to act.

The bear moved. The alder quivered. The man fired.

As big as the bear was, the man still missed, although the bullet raced by the bear's wounded shoulder. The man then checked his fire. The bear, still not appreciating the black stick, nevertheless had seen the man looking in its direction and heard a rare noise whiz by. The bear retreated and waited for the man to make the next move.

As soon as the man had fired the rifle, he had regretted doing so. Had he hit the bear it would have been a lucky shot, and in missing, the man effectively admitted that he didn't know exactly where the bear was. Worse than that, the man knew that the bear was alerted to his presence. And worst of all, whereas the man had at least a general idea of where the bear had been before he had fired the rifle, he presently had absolutely no idea where the bear was now.

In point of fact, the bear had already retreated about thirty yards and was now at the bottom of a small hill, effectively screened from the man by the alder and the hill. The bear had a choice of moving to the left and following the creek, moving to the right, or retreating. But after waiting all of these years, the bear would never retreat. The bear moved to the right and, in doing so, climbed up a small grade with the idea of circling around behind the man so as to hide in a tangle of tall grass that grew on a slight rise above the man's present position. If the man stayed where he was, the bear could get to within sixty yards of him while remaining completely hidden, and the bear could cover the remaining sixty yards in about four seconds.

The man felt naked, standing in the open, knowing that the bear was on the prowl but not knowing exactly where. Although the bear certainly had been gifted with the more discriminating senses, the man sensed that the bear wanted to kill him just as badly as he wanted to kill the bear.

The man considered his options, which numbered four. First, he could walk toward the alder thicket, but that would shorten the distance that the bear would have to charge, if the bear was still in the alder. Second, he could walk down to the creek, which would require him to surrender the high ground and, in exchange, gain nothing. Third, he could walk directly away from the alder thicket, which would still maintain his position above the creek. And fourth, he could walk farther up the hill to his left, toward a tangle of tall grass. Such an action would give him concealment from the bear's eyes but certainly not from its nose. But, such a position would still keep the man in control of the high ground. Regretting again his foolish discharge of the rifle, the man backed up the little rise toward the tangle of tall grass, unknowingly approaching the bear, which was already in place, watching the man move closer and closer. As the man drew closer to the bear, his hated scent grew stronger and stronger.

Just before the man got too close to the tangle of grass he realized that his occupying such a position would be safe enough, but only if the bear was not already there. The man realized that he had no idea as to where the bear was but knew that the bear would try and position itself so as to take advantage of the prevailing wind by keeping the man upwind. And, the best place for the bear to keep the man upwind would be in the tangle of grass that the man was about to enter. The man stopped just short of being too late, for the bear had already decided to make its move if the man got to the edge of the grass, and the man was only about thirty feet away. The light fog continued to drift around the man while he contemplated the possibilities. The man concluded that if the bear was in the grass, he would soon be dead unless he moved down the hill, away from the grass, back towards where he had been when he had let loose with the first shot.

It was a fascinating confrontation, superior intellect and modern weaponry being stalemated by natural instinct. The handicappers had been right, and the bear's ferocity had yet to even play a part.

The man had already made one mistake. But for all of his experience in the woods and in hunting game, the man now made his second mistake in assuming that the bear would make a mistake of its own. Mistakes are made by beings that can reason, by minds that can evaluate differing possibilities. So, while the man walked back down the hill and took up his original post, he assumed that the bear, in an attempt to keep the man upwind, would remain in the tangle of grass. The man hoped that, once lower on the hill, he could move to one side or the other until he had a clear shot at the bear that he felt to be in the tangle of grass.

The man felt secure enough in his spot, although the man also realized that he would not feel safe in that spot indefinitely, for it was already three thirty in the afternoon. In four hours' time it would be dusk. When the sun went down, whatever advantages the man possessed would be cancelled by the darkness. The rifle would be useless, and the man would have to focus his superior intellect and ability to reason not on killing the bear but on simply staying alive. The man assumed that the bear would stay in place, and this assumption was his second mistake. This was a bear that, while a creature of instinct, was displaying behavior inconsistent with its general nature.

The bear saw the man retreat back to where it had first seen him. Occupying its position in the tangle of grass, the bear waited for the man to act, but since the man had returned to his original position, he had not moved. The bear's instincts told it that its present position could be improved upon, and the bear, like the man had already done, quietly backed off, turned and waddled back to its original position in the alder, where the obstruction to the man's view was greater and where it could better monitor the man. There the bear waited. And while the bear waited in the alder thicket to the man's side, the man believed that the bear was in the tangle of grass on the top of the hill.

What had been three thirty in the afternoon soon was six forty-five in the evening, and the man knew that it was a half hour's walk back to his truck. The man knew that he would have to leave shortly and still believed that the bear was in the tangle of grass at the crest of the small hill. The man felt it fortunate that his truck was in a different direction from where he believed the bear to be. The man gathered what belongings he was going to carry and, with an eye to the tangle of grass to his left, set out for his truck that was parked not quite two miles distant, on the other side of the alder thicket where he had first felt the bear, on the other side of the alder thicket where the bear presently waited, ever watching the man as it slowly began walking toward him. As the man approached closer he loomed larger and larger. His odor became overpowering.

The man got to within thirty feet of the alder thicket, with one eye still checking the tangle of grass over his left shoulder while the other eye watched where he was going, when he realized that something wasn't right. It was a combination of things—the quiet of the birds, the stillness of the alder and other vague things that the man could not identify—that suggested to the man that he had not taken the bear seriously enough. Faster than he could describe, the man dropped his backpack, raised his rifle, unlocked its safety and pointed it into the alder thicket, but the man's actions were not fast enough. The bear came crashing through the thicket on a lope, shattering the quiet of the air and, when it hit the man, shattering his left arm.

The man was knocked to the ground, while the bear came to a stop twenty feet behind him. The man grabbed for his rifle but found that his left arm—his aiming arm—was broken and of no use. The man stared at the bear, rifle in hand, but unable to raise the rifle to take a shot.

The bear, for its part, wheeled around and faced the man. The bear was on all fours, with its front right paw stationary on the ground and his left front paw alternating from side to side of its right paw while it swung its massive body from side to side. The bear lowered its head but raised its snout and gave out a most hideous roar; half anger and half satisfaction, thought the man. The man looked down the nose of the bear and realized that he was doomed. The man knew that the bear would end its little dance at any moment and finish the job. The man thought that he had one or two seconds at most, but he made the most of them. The man raised the rifle with his right arm, held it at his hip, and pulled the trigger. The bear, still unaware of the significance of the black stick, felt the hot sharpness enter its left shoulder, not far from its twelve-year-old similar injury. The bear roared in pain and fell to the ground, and the man retreated into the alder, desperately trying to work the bolt mechanism of his rifle with one hand so as to reload for another shot.

It was still light where the man and the bear had their meeting just outside the alder thicket, but it was much darker inside the alder thicket. The man still had the rifle, but he was in no condition to use it. And it would be dark very soon. The man's time appeared to be quite limited, but he was able to work the action of his rifle until he had reloaded.

The man knew that he had hit the bear, but he didn't know how badly. And given his mistake from twelve years earlier, he was not about to approach the bear to find out. The man began to run through the woods, partly out of plan and partly out of panic. He frequently glanced over his shoulder to check and see if the bear was pursuing. The man decided that, if the bear gave chase, he would stop, turn, hold his ground and shoot again from the hip. That was really all he could do.

But the bear didn't pursue. Not immediately.

The bear was back just outside the alder thicket, where it had fallen. It was in agony from its new wound, and for the first time, it began to make a tenuous association between the pain in his shoulder and the black stick held by the man. The bear started to follow the man, but from a distance.

And so the two of them stumbled through the woods; the man running at top speed but with a crippled arm and the bear running at about the man's speed but on a crippled leg. One could not gain on the other. The man was too far ahead for the bear to catch, and the bear was too far behind for the man to have a clear shot. But as they covered the distance to the man's truck, the man began to tire, and the bear, noticing that it was getting closer, spurred itself on until the distance between them closed markedly. Now the bear was close enough for the man to shoot, but by now it was also too dark for the man to see what he would be shooting at. The man knew that he had to make good on his next shot, because if he missed, the bear would be on him before the man could reload the rifle with his crippled arm. Soon they arrived at the end of the trail, which led into a gravel pit, and in the far corner of the gravel pit, about one hundred yards away, was the man's truck.

The man raced for his truck, and the bear raced for the man. The distance between them was insignificant—fifty feet at most. The man realized that he might very well make it to his truck, but he would not have enough time to unlock the truck and climb in, for the bear was too close. The man knew that he would have to turn and shoot. Which he did.

The man's sudden stop and turn caught the bear off guard, and it was unable to stop in time. It crashed into the man, knocking him over. The man hit the ground, rolled upright, aimed his rifle as best as he could and pulled the trigger. The bear was about twenty feet away, facing the man, and standing on its hind legs.

The bullet left the muzzle at a dizzying velocity of over two thousand miles per hour. It hit the bear in its upper left chest, pierced its heart and lodged just off center in the bear's back. The bear's great heart, which had supplied the beast with life for eighteen years, sputtered and died. The bear, already approaching the man on its hind legs when it was hit, stumbled an additional several feet, but not in control of itself, for it was already dead in all but word. It took two steps with its left rear paw alternating with a single step of its right rear paw and collapsed forward. All five hundred pounds of Ursus americanus fell atop Homo sapiens, and in the process crushed the latter's two lungs, two kidneys, liver, pancreas and heart. Homo sapiens suffocated under the weight of Ursus americanus.

Two great hunters perished on a foggy, rainy evening on the second day of the third week of September in the Superior National Forest. Each, in the special way of its own kind, had been driven by an overpowering desire, and each, again in the special way of its own kind, satisfied that desire, and both in the exact same way paid the ultimate price.

WELL, EXCUUUSE ME

On February 17 of a year you'll have to guess at, we were camped on the north shore of Daniels Lake, only a hop-skip into the Boundary Waters from Hungry Jack Lodge, which is just off of the Gunflint Trail. On both the day before and the day of our entry the weather gods had blessed us (or cursed us, you get to decide) with three inches of snow. Six inches of white powder made for a most exquisite sight, but it made the pulling of our toboggans all the more arduous. We stopped at the first flat spot we found and began the process of setting up a winter camp: flattening down and filling in the tent pad, pitching the tent, guying it, tightening it, making it just so, putting in the stove and making it level and then drilling a hole in the ice for water, all before finally getting around to dealing with everybody's (least) favorite winter camping chore: collecting firewood.

All other things being equal, the success or miserableness of a winter trip turns on the quality and quantity of the firewood. Some of my friends, Jim and Bob in particular, are wood wizards, and I know that, however cold I am during the day, I'll be warm and comfortable in the tent at night if Jim or Bob is on the crew.

My wood hunting skills are hit and miss—sometimes I am lucky and fortunate to find plenty of good wood, and other times I am lucky and fortunate to have Jim or Bob along for the ride.

At this particular camp we had a nice supply of good wood, but after a few days our supply was dwindling fast, so armed with my collapsible saw and amputation-ready ax, I began my quest for more.

There are many trees in the forest, and sometimes it's hard to find what you're seeking: something tall, standing, no green, no longer alive, ideally a black ash, although other species of trees will work just fine. For example, setting up a winter camp next to a cedar swamp will make one about as comfortable as setting up camp in one's bedroom.

After about fifteen minutes of trudging through the knee-high sugar snow, I found a likely candidate. The tree was proudly standing upright, and it had no green about it. I hit the tree's trunk with the poll of my ax, and it felt solid. I shook it—or attempted to—but it did not budge. I blazed the trunk with the ax blade, placed my thumb on the cut face and felt the heat from my thumb reflecting back from the wood—a dependable indication that it was dry. I put down my ax, and after assembling my saw, I went to work.

I started with a horizontal cut about twelve inches above the snow. At first, no problems. Then I was showered by a light burst of snow that fell from the upper branches. Nothing out of the ordinary there. I continued to saw away, and then a few clumps of snow, and then even larger clumps of snow, tumbled down. My anorak's hood was not up, and a big clump of snow hit me square on the neck.

"Pretty cold," I thought to myself, followed by, "pretty wet, too."

I continued to slave away and my back and forth sawing motion apparently loosened some branches from higher up, because all of a sudden I was pelted with falling pieces of wood of all shapes and sizes—enough for a fine pile of kindling, some larger chunks and even some bigger pieces that would have to be split before they could be added to the fire. I was beginning to get the idea that maybe I should not be working on this tree at all, but we needed more firewood, so I droned on, sawing away, until I dislodged a final piece of wood. This last piece to fall was large enough to hold a jacked-up car in place. It hit me on my right shoulder, and it hurt. Bad. Throwing down my saw, I stood up, I looked up, I raised my voice up, and I got ready to swear.

But before I could utter a single expletive, I was grabbed under each arm by two long, stringy branches and hoisted eighteen feet into the air. I was pulled, up close and personal, to the trunk of the tree, and before being tossed aside into a snowdrift, where I landed head first and hip deep with my legs sticking up like a double lollipop, what I thought had been a knothole in the tree's trunk opened up and in loud, low, growling, disgusting, condescending words, said to me, **"I'M NOT DEAD YET."**

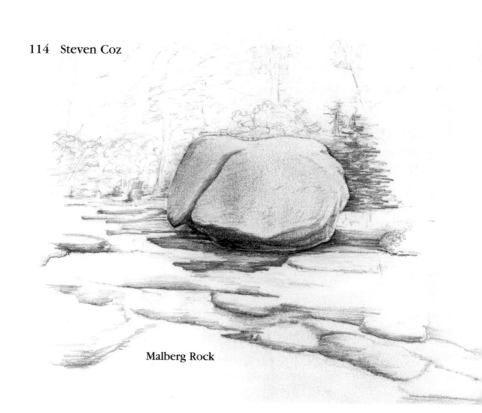

Malberg Rock

Phoebe River Balancing Boulders

WHADDYA MEAN I CAN'T HAVE A MOTOR ON THIS LAKE?

and, by the way,

WHERE DID THIS LAKE COME FROM ANYWAY?

(A short geological and political history of the Boundary Waters)

Two excellent questions posed by a fictitious camper that I will christen Jill, named after a dog musher friend of mine that I'm thinking about right now, although I can't imagine that Jill would ever own an outboard motor in the first place. Jill is about to experience a wilderness environment unlike anything else in our very big country. Not even in Alaska will Jill find what she is about to discover. How did this area come to be in the first place? What primordial forces created this interconnected series of waterways? And what workings of man have led to it being purposely undeveloped? Human nature, as a seminal TV series in the late 1960s suggested, is to "boldly go where no man has gone before." How were people and developers kept out?

a) A geological history of the Boundary Waters

On the southern tip of Malberg Lake there rests an enormous boulder, sitting all by itself. It is huge, but it is not unique. Unknown to everyone that has never seen it, it must seem odd to anyone coming across it for the first time because it seems so out of place. At ten feet high and sixteen feet wide and weighing several tons, it dwarfs anything around. It sits on an outcropping of flat rock towards the bottom of a stream. It just doesn't belong there. But there it is. I have christened it the "Malberg Rock."

On the Phoebe River, on the way from Phoebe Lake to Lake Polly, two people in a tandem canoe will come across two large boulders, neither anywhere near as large as the Malberg Rock, but in combination they are just as fascinating, for these two boulders are balancing, one atop the other. The smaller of the two boulders—the one on top—by several times outweighs anything that many canoeists could pick up and move around. The boulders sit above the floodplain, which means that the spring runoff had nothing to do with placing the smaller boulder atop the larger one.

Only a glacier could have left these two rocks in their peculiar arrangement. Only a glacier could explain the Malberg Rock. And glaciers have not visited northeastern Minnesota for at least ten thousand years.

But any geological discussion of the Boundary Waters has to begin much earlier than ten thousand years ago. A good place to start is with the Canadian Shield.

Imagine a huge, fat *U* on a map, with the base anchored on northern Minnesota, the left arm curling in a northwesterly direction all the way to the Arctic Ocean and the right arm curling in a northeasterly direction covering all of Quebec and Labrador and only stopping at the North Atlantic, and you have the Canadian Shield. The rock that makes up the Canadian Shield is Precambrian, and at three billion years old, among the oldest on Earth. The Boundary Waters Canoe Area Wilderness sits atop the Canadian Shield and this ancient rock, stretching about 115 miles along the Minnesota-Ontario border.

The many lakes found in the Boundary Waters were formed by glacial activity during the last of the four ice ages that Earth has experienced. Glaciers are large, slow-moving rivers of ice that are pulled along by gravity and are formed by snow that collects faster than it melts. At the bottom of the glacier, a sole of ice melts under the tremendous weight of the ice above it, and the glacier slides along this sole. "Slides" is probably a misleading word to use, for the movement of a glacier is anything but smooth. In point of fact, the glacier scrapes and scratches and gouges the underlying rock as it moves along at an unbelievably slow pace. How slow? Depending on variables such as size, temperature and slope, a glacier may move as little as six millimeters per hour (one quarter inch per hour). A snail moves faster. Along the way glaciers pick up and accumulate all sorts of debris, only to deposit the debris as they start to shrink and recede. In doing this, glaciers mold the surface of the Earth.

Evidence of glacier movement can be seen on the face of the exposed rock in the Boundary Waters. Striations are parallel lines scratched into the surface of a rock, suggesting that another rock was stuck or frozen into the base of the glacier as it moved. Wider, deeper markings on the rock faces are known as grooves. As a glacier advances it picks up anything in its path that is loose, and deposits its collection in many ways. The Malberg Rock is an example of a glacial erratic. Erratics are single rocks deposited far from their source. The two boulders on the Phoebe River are also examples of glacial erratics, and their balancing act is an interesting subject to contemplate while having lunch in a canoe. Along the margins of the glacier, sediment gathers and settles and forms uneven terrain. Chains of lakes frequently form along these margins.

Ten to twelve thousand years ago our area was covered by glaciers. The glaciers stripped away all traces of topsoil and soft rock deposits and left barren rock. Melting glaciers, the underground water table and melting snow then filled the low lying areas, forming the lakes. The ice ground down and plucked away old weathered and fractured rock, deepened existing valleys, rounded off ridges and scratched the remaining rock. More resistant rock was not so easily eroded by glacial activity and forms most of the bedrock hills we see today. Other hills were formed by glacial deposits of rock and soil.

Although Earth has been covered by huge sheets of ice at least four times, what we see today are the effects of the last visit by glaciers to northern Minnesota, with the last glaciers leaving about ten thousand years ago.

After the glaciers receded they left behind a tangle of interconnected rivers and streams and hundreds of lakes, providing an ideal canoe country. The Laurentian Divide between the Great Lakes and the Hudson Bay watersheds runs northeast-southwest through the east side of the Boundary Waters. Lakes and rivers to the north of the divide drain to Hudson Bay and the Arctic Ocean, while other lakes and rivers to the south ultimately empty out in the Atlantic Ocean.

Exposed bedrock dominates the border lakes area, distinguishing the area from other parts of Minnesota. This region is unlike the rest of the state, which is almost completely covered by glacial deposits, and that explains why there are so many rock-rimmed lakes in the Boundary Waters. Because of the glaciation of the Ice Age and the characteristic Precambrian rock of northeast Minnesota, the border lakes area has the highest concentration of lakes in the state, which in turn has the most lakes of any state.

But getting back to the Malberg Rock—what is *its* story? No one knows much, other than the Malberg Rock and the two boulders balancing on the Phoebe River have been in place for about ten thousand years. If you ever find yourself in the presence of the Malberg Rock or the twin boulders of the Phoebe River, take a moment to reflect on just how long these pieces of history have been in place— I know that Jill will. Like a meteorite that has fallen to Earth, their origins are not meant to be known, and where they came from is anybody's guess.

b) A political history of the Boundary Waters

If you live in northeastern Minnesota and spend any time in the woods, you are probably aware of the long-running and oftentimes bitter debate over the Boundary Waters Canoe Area Wilderness and how it should be used and enjoyed. Our local treasure—only a few hours' drive away, and for some, only fifteen minutes away—continuously sparred over by people who want to use it but who cannot agree on how it should be used. Each side staking out the moral high ground. Maybe you've even picked a side to support.

Pro-motor groups vs. no-motor groups. Environmentalists vs. loggers. Developers vs. conservationists. A limit on group size. The requirement of having a permit when travelling in the King's Forest. Restrictions on the number of permits issued. Plastic bottles being allowed, but glass bottles being verboten, even though both litter the countryside quite effectively. A well-known environmental group based in a big city a few hundred miles away acting in good faith to protect the wilderness but putting working parents of small children out of work in the process. A significantly-sized ecostructure made "off-limits" to anybody unwilling or unable to conform their behavior to federally-mandated requirements imposed by people who don't live here. A desire to protect one of the few remaining wild areas in our country—a singular canoe wilderness unknown anyplace else in the United States—relatively untouched by the same forces that bring jobs and schools and hospitals. Management's stated goal to preserve the wilderness by insisting that its users "leave no trace" but then installing two thousand fire grates and two thousand fiberglass latrines and demanding that they be used. An Englishman two generations ago, while observing development of wild and wilderness areas in the United States, commented that we Americans were "fools, destroying their heritage." Many people would respond that a resident of a foreign country thousands of miles away has no dog in this fight and that he should keep his opinions to himself.

Very tough issues—no easy answers.

Things never got to an all-out civil war—we have not yet had our own Fort Sumter, shots haven't been fired*—but there certainly were, and there still certainly remain, lots of bad feelings between members of the two competing groups, one of which might be said to favor unrestricted access and use so as to benefit the largest number of people, while the other might be said to favor restricted access and use so as to enhance the experience of those who appreciate solitude; one of which groups my brother belongs to, while I support the other.

How did we get to this point? The natives that lived here before the French-Canadian voyageurs first arrived in the late 1600s certainly didn't live by a system of permits and daily quotas, but many people will be surprised to learn that the voyageurs themselves were eventually required to have permits issued by the authorities in Montreal

---

*In 2008, several adults and juveniles were prosecuted for terrorizing campers by shooting firearms and threatening acts of violence during an isolated incident that occurred on a Boundary Waters lake in Lake County. At least one of the individuals involved offered as an explanation for his behavior the restrictions on use of the wilderness imposed from afar by people in positions of authority.

before they could traffic in beaver pelts—a requirement to have a permit in the Boundary Waters is nothing new. The routes that we paddle, ski and snowshoe today are the same routes used by generations of Sioux and by generations of Chippewa after them. At the time the first white man paddled through what eventually came to be the Boundary Waters, the Sioux represented the dominant civilization in northeastern Minnesota, except for the Arrowhead region of Minnesota, which was settled by the Chippewa. The Sioux were slowly and gradually pushed westward to the plains and prairies by advancing Chippewa from the east, who were in turn greatly aided by firearms obtained from whites advancing even farther from the east. As legacies, the Sioux and later the Chippewa left behind both the abstract and the tangible: abstract names of various lakes and tangible painted rocks depicting events that we can only hazard an educated guess at as to their meaning. Both the lake names and the painted rocks survive to this day.

The area had remained unmolested and unchanged for eons except for the workings of Nature, and Nature generally works at a much, much slower pace than man. But when Jacques de Noyon became the first white man to travel through the area in 1688, he brought with him change, and change took root very quickly. Fur traders began to travel the canoe routes in the 1700s, trapping beaver whose pelts would make fine top hats for gentlemen in Europe. By the mid-1770s the legendary voyageurs were making their mark. Arriving from Montreal in enormous birch bark canoes, they brought trade goods for distribution to the northern interior of the continent and left with pelts from beaver, otter and muskrat, but mostly beaver.

Eventually the fur traders brought with them organized businesses in the form of the North West Company and the Hudson's Bay Company—bitter enemies in the war for fur—and then things developed at an even quicker pace, as the companies competed against one another for supremacy of a land rich in animal pelts. Tiny outposts like Fort William and York Factory became competing Romes of a fur empire, and for a few weeks in the fall of any given year they became the focus of activity of the continent's interior as voyageurs came to deliver pelts they had obtained from the natives deeper within the continent.

Perennially warring nations England and France fought each other in the French and Indian War, but by 1760, France had lost and what was to eventually become known as the Dominion of Canada became a colony of England. English outposts replaced those of the French, but vigorous competition between the rival fur companies continued. However, soon after the turn of the century the fur trade, which had been instrumental in bringing people and development to the area, began to wind down. The reasons behind the precipitous decline in the fur trade were simple: the competition between the two companies was fierce, the War of 1812 led to the destruction of outposts and equipment, and trade routes had become overextended.

In 1842, the United States and England signed the Webster-Ashburton Treaty and in the process established the international border between the United States and Canada. The border between present-day Minnesota and Ontario was set more-or-less by following the dominant canoe trade route to the west, now known as the Voyageur's Highway. The Treaty of La Pointe in 1854 between the United States and the Chippewa of Lake Superior opened eastern Minnesota to further exploration and development.

After the Civil War, northeastern Minnesota absorbed an influx of people, mainly farmers, miners and loggers, and the railroads soon followed. False gold rushes led to crushed hopes for many people, but the discovery of enormous deposits of iron ore and hematite led to the establishment of numerous cities and towns located next to open pit and underground mines. Mining and logging companies greatly expanded upon the work of individuals.

In 1895 the first chief fire warden of Minnesota, Christopher C. Andrews, called for the preservation of Minnesota's forests for later generations. Joined by citizens from the Twin Cities, he began a campaign that in 1902 led to the establishment of a 200,000-acre forest in north central Minnesota that later became the Chippewa National Forest.

Shortly thereafter Andrews began a similar campaign in northeastern Minnesota but achieved little success with the Minnesota legislature. Andrews then sought help from the federal government and achieved great success. Over the course of the next six years the federal government, under the leadership of President Theodore Roosevelt, set aside 1,100,000 acres of land that in 1909 was officially designated as the Superior National Forest. The following years witnessed the expansion of the Superior National Forest and the establishment of a rudimentary highway system in the United States that promoted travel. More people began to realize the benefits of recreation, and use of the Superior National Forest increased.

In 1926, a portion of the Superior National Forest about one thousand acres in size was preserved as a roadless area, and this was expanded in the 1930s. Public support for the preservation of the area's natural beauty increased, and in the late 1920s policies were adopted in an attempt to manage the growing wilderness area. The main focus of these policies was to retain as much wilderness as possible.

But this initial establishment and subsequent expansions were not done without protest or objection; for every conservationist wanting to save, there was a developer wanting to build. Resorts began appearing in the area, and proposals were made to put in a road through the heart of the wilderness all the way east to the Gunflint Trail. Some developers wanted a road to every lake in the area, and there were over two hundred lakes to be considered. Hydroelectric dams were proposed and defeated, and some restrictions on logging and mining were enacted. In 1930, Congress enacted the Shipstead-Newton-Nolan Act, which had far-reaching effects. The act called for the conservation of shorelines for boat and canoe travel, the prohibition of logging within four hundred feet of natural shorelines and a prohibition against tampering with natural water levels.

In 1939, the original area and its subsequent enlargements, still "roadless," were designated as such, and the Superior Roadless Primitive Area came into being. This area, then totaling approximately one million acres in size, more or less established the present boundaries of what, in 1958, became known as the Boundary Waters Canoe Area. Management of this federally owned land became the responsibility of the Cabinet-level Department of Agriculture, in general, and its subdivision, the United States Forest Service, in particular.

The Wilderness Act of 1964 designated the Boundary Waters Canoe Area as a part of the National Wilderness Preservation System, and special regulations adopted in 1965 established management priorities that are still followed to this day. Ely, a small community ("not the end of the road, but you can see it from there") that is presently considered by many to be the gateway to the Boundary Waters, was in the 1960s still a mining town.

In the mid-1970s environmentalists began advocating for more laws—more restrictions on mining and motors and an outright ban on logging—to protect the area that was being threatened, not only by development, but by wilderness tourism itself. Suddenly everyone wanted to go canoe camping in northeastern Minnesota. In 1978, Congress enacted the Boundary Waters Canoe Area Wilderness (BWCAW) Act. In doing so, Congress granted wilderness status to the Boundary Waters Canoe Area. This resulted in an outright prohibition against logging, mining and most motor use in an area that at that time was heavily logged, heavily mined and pervaded with outboard motors.

Ely was caught in the middle. Many residents made a living and supported their children by mining, logging and guiding in the wilderness with motors. Many residents of Ely objected to restrictions imposed by the federal government located a thousand miles away, restrictions proposed and advocated by people who lived far away.

Passage of the 1978 BWCAW Act was preceded and followed by many burnings in effigy of politicians and environmentalists. Congressman Bruce Vento and wilderness icon Sigurd Olson both come to mind, but there were many others. Passage of the 1978 BWCAW Act also resulted in the outright immediate ban of motors on many lakes, an eventual ban of motors on other lakes, and the establishment of limits on the size of motors on yet other lakes. Individuals and small businesses that catered to people using motors, either outboards on boats in the summer or snowmobiles in the winter, were put out of work or put out of business. Canoeists arriving in Ely by car were stopped and asked to sign petitions. Passage of the 1978 BWCAW Act also led to the buying out of resorts located within the Boundary Waters. I had lunch at the Sawbill Lodge after one of my very first trips to the Boundary Waters—I was probably one of the last people to do so.

So where are we now?

People that were put out of work by federally mandated restrictions have either adapted or moved away. Ely is no longer an unknown mining town but rather the jumping off point for people from fifty states that make the city popular beyond the level that its small size suggests. Wilderness canoe travel has become a thriving business in its own right, and the Boundary Waters presently sees perhaps more people than it should—a few years ago the Forest Service reduced the maximum number of people in any given group to nine. The number of permits available for entry at the various official entry points has decreased, as have the number of campsites. Nevertheless, canoeists that want to travel in the wilderness and not see a soul will be disappointed; in 2008, there were 136,000 visitors to the Boundary Waters, and although the numbers are down from 157,000 in 2003, the area remains the most popular and most visited wilderness area in the United States. A lottery had to be enacted to address the demand for permits at the more popular entry points. But my friend Jill has 1,200 miles of canoe routes to explore when she comes. She can do so without interference from mining companies, loggers or developers. And she won't see any railroads either.

But, what if you are *not* a canoeist? What if you like to troll in a motorboat? Or what if you like to run a snowmobile across a virgin winter lake? Or what if you are disabled and cannot walk a portage at all? And what if you are a young couple with twin toddlers? Many people still chafe at the restrictions, and although the vast majority honor them, an occasional renegade snowmobile can still be seen illegally operating where legally it cannot. Intentional killing of timber wolves—*the* wilderness icon—is not unheard of. Several years ago, a coward unwilling to identify himself mailed to the Outdoors writer of the *Duluth News Tribune* the severed head of a timber wolf just to prove a point, although whatever point he was trying to prove remains elusive.

Environmentalists and conservationists take great pride in believing that they are playing a role in keeping the Boundary Waters in the same state that it has always been in; a state of ancient forests and unexplored wilderness. Yet many of them would be surprised to learn that the Boundary Waters that most people are personally familiar with today is not the Boundary Waters of old. Forest fires and clear-cutting have done away with great swaths of red pine and white pine, to be replaced with spruce, balsam, jack pine and aspen and the different animals that flourish with the new growth. People who desire to preserve the Boundary Waters in a state that they believe has always existed are simply trying to preserve the Boundary Waters in the state that they prefer. Perhaps the best argument against preservation and conservation is simply this: Nature acts very slowly, but Nature does act. The Boundary Waters has always been in flux, and trying to preserve it in a particular state ignores all the other states that it has naturally occupied. Who are we to say which state is better than any of the others?

But, getting back to the question: "What if you are *not* a canoeist?" Have all of these regulations really accomplished anything? Several years ago I traveled north on Sawbill Lake with my wife and two friends. As I steered the canoe from the stern I recalled the very first time I had been on Sawbill Lake; about twenty years earlier I had been sitting in the bow of a canoe steered by a special friend that I have since fallen out of touch with. I looked at the shoreline on the east side of the lake, and I realized that very little had changed over the past twenty years. This was a good thing. It was heartening to believe that the lake would look pretty much the same in another twenty years, and maybe indefinitely.

Every few years one side or the other proposes enlarging or curtailing the Boundary Waters. Tempers rise, lawyers are hired, letters to the editor increase, each side digs in and half-truths are spread. Money and dirty politics have been utilized by all of the players. "Wise use" advocates complain about government interference exercised from afar, and conservationists deplore the shortsightedness of their opponents. Snowmobilers worry about having even fewer trails on which to ride, while canoeists worry about having even fewer lakes to paddle, and people caught in the middle worry about their children and their jobs.

It really is beyond dispute and debate: present regulations do deny a significant percentage of the local population unfettered use of the Boundary Waters and keep many people from practicing their preferred professions. On the other hand, there really are some natural treasures that, once gone, really are gone forever. And forever means forever. There are moral absolutes in life—things that are right or wrong, and not for any particular reason, but just because they are. Moral absolutes. My sense is that the preservation of a rare wilderness area is one of them.

It might be accurate to suggest that, after a hundred years of bickering, an uneasy balance has finally been achieved and that both sides, without ever publicly admitting it, really do realize that the present arrangement, which permits virtually unrestricted use of millions of acres of land, while severely restricting the use of one million acres of land, does seem to accommodate most of the people involved. Not perfectly, to be sure, but well enough.

THE LAKE POLLY BEAR
(Part II)

So my bride of twenty-five years and I were hung up on this large, flat, barely-submerged, Kevlar-attracting slab of granite just north of the Kawasachong Lake narrows. We, along with Dan and Mary, were headed north—destination Lake Polly, the site of this year's annual canoe trip. Somehow Dan and Mary had avoided this Precambrian-era risk to navigation that now held us fast. Strong and forceful paddling strokes and a few colorful words of encouragement to my bride had done little to free us. To complicate matters, the westerly wind had increased to just shy of gale force levels and *Tinker Bell*, my Minnesota II Kevlar canoe—so named because it is so light on my shoulders—was slowly spinning like a pinwheel, and as I sat in the stern encouraging my bride with even more sharply directed epithets, I kept an eye on the bottom of my boat, watching for the tip of rock to slowly drill through *Tinker Bell*'s hull, the sight of which would visibly announce the commencement of our inevitable sinking.

I could see Dan and Mary on the shoreline, commingled among the other groups going in and coming out of the Boundary Waters. Forest Service regulations prohibit more than nine people in any given location in the wilderness, but to me it looked like there were nine separate *groups* at the portage, and God only knows how many people. And two of those people had just put in and were heading our way.

This trip, like all other trips that originate at the Forest Service Station in Tofte, had begun with dire warnings from the resident ranger about the Lake Polly Bear. Dan and I had feigned rapt attention to the ranger's words but secretly smiled at each other as we recalled our confrontation, just shy of four years ago, with the Lake Polly Beaver. We paid little attention to today's warnings that, in retrospect, really were a bit more ominous than those of years past.

But that was several hours ago, and now, as my better half and I were stuck on a hidden rock, we were approached by two paddlers in a tandem canoe. My bride suggested that we ask for help, but I was not yet ready to concede that my sorry navigational skills had deposited us into a situation that required outside assistance, so I said, "No, we'll get off of this thing on our own."

However, my bride had apparently tired of dealing with my pride, for the next thing I heard was a voice from the front of *Tinker Bell*, imploringly pleading, "Can you help us?"

The response, "Sure, we'll help you off of that rock," told me that my opportunity to save face by saving ourselves had been taken from me. It was already shaping up to be a long trip.

Our savior-to-be, Max, still seated in the stern of the friendly canoe, put one foot on the rock and grabbed *Tinker Bell*'s gunnel and pulled, and like magic, we were free! We thanked Max profusely (my bride's offerings of gratitude were a bit more zealously delivered than mine, as I was still nursing my injured pride). That's when Max inquired of us as to our destination, and when we responded, "Lake Polly," the following exchange more-or-less took place:

Max: Don't camp on Lake Polly.

Us: Why?

Max: Too many bears!

Me: I've dealt with the Lake Polly Bear before—it's no big thing. In fact, it's not even a bear. It's a beav…

Max: People have had their packs torn. Shredded ropes are hanging from trees. It's not safe.

Me: We'll be careful.

Max: A few nights ago a group had a bear in their camp. Instead of fleeing from the campers, the bear had taken a run at one of them. And after eating their food, the bear went to sleep twenty feet from the tent and snored throughout the night. Children were traumatized.

Me: Well, thanks again for your help.

Max and his disciple, Peter, who was manning the bow, paddled off, but not before Max yelled out over his shoulder, "Don't camp on Polly. Keep going. Go up to Koma. Or better yet, don't stop until you get to Malberg."

My bride and I paddled to the northern shore of Kawasachong and met up with Dan and Mary. Distressingly, they, too, had been accosted with bear stories. Between what Max had told us and what the other campers had told our friends, it began to sound like there were roving street gangs of marauding bears all over the perimeter of Lake Polly—the Campsite 11 Big Bad Bruins, the North Polly Cubby Boys, the Gangsta Bears, and Smokey's Revenge. Bears in long, baggy pants, wearing baseball caps sideways. The image was too much for me.

We were one long portage, a tiny lake and another garden variety portage away from the southern tip of Lake Polly, and as we began the walk-paddle-walk process that would bring us to our destination, we all started to think about what we had been told. I had intended to politely ignore the warnings that we had received from the ranger that had issued us our permit in Tofte—I had been hearing about the Lake Polly Bear for decades—and the rumors of bears charging campers and sleeping outside of tent doors sounded like so much exaggeration. But I kept coming back to Max. In the five minutes that I had spent with Max—paying attention to how he was dressed, observing how he had handled his canoe, checking over his gear and enviously admiring his composure, I had concluded that Max was one very experienced canoe camper who knew his stuff. I wasn't about to accept his advice willy-nilly and pass straight through to Malberg Lake, but by the time we reached Lake Polly I had decided that maybe there really was something to these bear stories. The shredded rope that we saw dangling from a campsite that we passed didn't help matters.

Dan had apparently come to the same conclusion, because when we got to our site on the northern end of Lake Polly, we began to talk about what to do with our food. As we were making camp I realized that we were only about a quarter mile south of our encounter with the Lake Polly Beaver from four years ago. While putting up our tent I recalled to myself a tale relayed to me years earlier of a bear on another lake. Rumor had it that food packs were mysteriously disappearing at the Alton Lake/Beth Lake portage, and a canoe camper decided to get to the bottom of things. He unloaded his canoe, left the food pack on the ground, hoisted the canoe onto his shoulders, and started to portage to the west, but after about one hundred yards he quietly put his canoe down and stealthily snuck back to the beginning of the portage, where he waited. His patience was rewarded by the sight of a bear that snuck out of the brush, grabbed the food pack, and dove back into the woods. The canoe camper followed the bear through the tangled foliage until he came to a clearing in the woods, and there, to his amazement, was a veritable depot of food packs—rows and rows and columns and columns of food packs, stacked four or five high! It is said that all good legends are based on fact, and although I really didn't accept the "food pack depot" story at face value, it was not inconceivable to me that a bear would know when to strike, make off with someone's vittles and take his catch to his favorite spot.

It was apparent that our tried and true, never yet failed method—wrapping the food packs in a tarp and leaving them by the fire grate—just might not be the right thing to do this time 'round. The campsite that we had chosen was blessed, not with a tree to hang a pack from, but rather with a small island about a ninety-second paddle away from us. Although bears have been bestowed with the finest sense of smell in the entire animal kingdom, they are also creatures of habit, and we were confident that any bears in the area would be looking upward—towards the sky—towards the tops of the trees that the Forest Service tells us to hang our food packs from. We concluded that no bear would swim to a small island and look for food when all he or she would have to do would be to climb the same tree in the same campsite and relieve some campers of their food. So after our first night's dinner, we paddled to the small island directly across from our campsite, found a depression in the soft, fragrant moss, placed the food packs in the depression, wrapped the packs with the tarp, and paddled back to our campsite.

When we awoke the next morning all was right with the world. No guests had visited our campsite during the night, and the food packs, safely ensconced on the small island, had remained unmolested. We retrieved our food, breakfasted, did the dishes, packed up the food and paddled it to the island, returned to our campsite and sat back and listened to the wind, which told us to "stay in camp today." By then the campsite chipmunk had become quite friendly, although the campsite red squirrel was being aloof. And of course, the campsite Whiskey Jacks that had been assigned to this campsite were sitting in the trees, surveying their domain.

The day passed without incident and when the dinner hour rolled around, we got the food packs, prepared dinner and ate. By the time we returned the food packs to the island, now known as the "food storage facility," the sun was resting on the horizon. It was another pleasant evening in the Boundary Waters, lengthened by the great stash of dead wood that we retrieved from the island for our campfire. We retired and went to bed and slept peacefully, secure with the knowledge that our food was safe from hungry bears.

Tuesday morning began as a repeat of Monday's, with us going for the food and cooking up a nice, aromatic breakfast of pancakes, bacon and eggs, after which the dishes were done, the camp was cleaned up, things were organized and my bride walked down a path to the water's edge to brush her teeth. It was at about that time that I had decided that maybe we had overreacted by going to the trouble of taking our food to the island. After all, we had now been in camp for two days and two nights, and there had been no sign of the Lake Polly Bear.

It was then that I heard a strange sound from the general direction in which teeth were being brushed. Dan had heard something too, because he was looking in the same direction that I was. We then saw my bride running back up the trail to the campsite, frothing white at the mouth (from toothpaste or fear I am still not sure) and then the word "bear" bubbled out of her mouth. For added effect, the word "bear" bubbled out of her mouth a second time. By now she was behind me, relatively safe, and the four of us were looking down the trail, but seeing nothing.

My bride is not the world's best historian, but she is also not given to fits of hysterical behavior either, so I was…I was…what was I? I was…curious about what she had seen. Apparently so was Dan, for he had grabbed two canoe paddles and was obviously intending to walk down the trail. Not to be outdone, I grabbed the lids of two kettles (they looked like black Mountain Safety Research cymbals) and prepared to follow Dan down the trail.

As we took our first steps, seeking the cause of my bride's excitement, I asked myself, "Why am I doing this?" I thought about the potential matchup between Steve and the Lake Polly Bear. Logic would suggest that I should not actively seek out a wild animal much stronger, much faster and much hungrier than I was. On my side of the equation I could rely on my supposedly superior intellect, although the fact that I was actively seeking out a wild beast with nothing but cooking utensils for weapons did seem to suggest that I had already forfeited my claim to superior intelligence, if I had ever possessed it in the first place. Of course, as a bonus I could also rely on that one attribute that makes humans the envy of the rest of the animal kingdom, opposable thumbs, although I was not sure how opposable thumbs would assist me in a fight to the death with the beast. But it then occurred to me that I really didn't have to outfight or even outrun the bear—I'd only have to outrun Dan, and that would be an easy thing to do, because if there really was a bear down the trail, and if the bear gave chase, I would have a dry trail to run on, whereas Dan, who would have been behind me on the return trip, would not.

We started down the trail, Dan clacking the paddles, and me accompanying him on the MSR cymbals, sounding like a two-man, marching Boundary Waters percussion band. Ginger Baker, Max Weinberg, Gene Krupa, Buddy Rich—those guys had nothing on us! Of course, the trail was empty of what we sought, so we returned to the campsite, swiveling our heads to watch our backs on the return trip.

About twenty minutes later I was charged with the responsibility of getting rid of the dirty dishwater ("You *shall* dispose of the dishwater, because I'm not going down in that direction again"), so I made my way down the trail, kettle of dirty water in hand, where, at the water's edge, I would take a sharp turn to the left and walk into the woods. Just before reaching the water's edge there was a large tree blocking the trail that one had to step over to continue. Just as I got to the tree, I noticed, on the other side, what appeared to be a large Newfoundland dog (for you non-canine people, picture a coal-black St. Bernard). How odd, I said to myself—what in the world is a Newfoundland doing there?

I have read that, when a bear is angry or upset or thinking about acting out of character, it will start to huff. The bear huffed, turned and ambled in the other direction. I turned and ambled back to the campsite, leaving a wet trail behind me. When I got to the campsite the word "bear" bubbled out of my mouth. For added effect, the word "bear" bubbled out of my mouth a second time.

So, the legendary Lake Polly Bear was more than a legend after all.

Our campsite was now on full alert, with me observing the trail that I had just been on, Dan eyeing a different trail leading to the other side of the campsite, and Mary and my bride making noises with whatever was within reach.

All of a sudden Dan yelled out, "Bear!" Sure enough, the bear had circled around us and was now approaching our campsite from the opposite direction. Or was it? I know that bears are fast, but that was a lot of territory for the Newfoundland bear to cover in a short amount of time. My God, it occurred to me, we are the victims of a coordinated assault! There was more than one bear! The North Polly Cubby Boys were out in force! They are going to hit us from two different directions at the same time. Except that, there was still the trail to the latrine exactly between the two trails on which bears had already been sighted. We were about to be hit from three directions at the same time! I thought of how George Meade must have felt commanding the Army of the Potomac at Gettysburg so many years ago: first he held off the attacks of Heth and Ewell on the right, the following day he barely, and I mean barely (no pun intended), repulsed Longstreet on his left, and then, up the center, the next day, came Pickett's Charge. Were we about to be the target of a frontal assault, with flanking attacks to preoccupy us? I glanced down and wondered how much time we would have before the four of us were seated on the fire grate, each one of us facing a different direction, each of us leaning backwards against the others, each of us providing to the others whatever support we could, as we awaited the final, multidirectional assault. Perhaps the Lake Polly Beaver from four years ago would waddle down the quarter mile to our campsite and gloat.

But, of course, it didn't happen.

Dan's bear—which was my Newfoundland bear, which was also my bride's toothpaste bear—had turned and sauntered away, apparently concluding that these four humans and their food were not worth the trouble.

The rest of the trip passed without incident, although there were a few times when someone stepped out from a place in which he or she was not expected, to the surprise of the shocked party. Whenever one of us went up the trail to the biffy we carried a roll of toilet paper in one hand and two black MSR cymbals in the other hand. And I could not quite get over the feeling that there were two little beady eyes staring at me from behind the bushes, drilling tiny holes in the small of my back, while their owner, still hungry, bided his time....

ADDENDUM

So, what should campers do with their food?

Bears are not unintelligent. Bears know where the "good" trees are at a campsite. Hanging the food pack gets the food off the ground and in the open air, where the breezes spread the odors around in all directions. And remember, bears have the most acute sense of smell in the animal kingdom. Bears are expert tree climbers. And bears, like all wild animals, are not impatient and have more time to outwit you than you have to outwit them. If a bear sees your food pack, he won't give up until he has it or until you depart your campsite. Hanging your food pack from a convenient tree is the same thing as putting a letter in the mailbox and then raising the red flag to tell the mailman that there's a letter waiting to be picked up.

If you must hang your food pack, do not use the obvious tree close to the campsite. The bear knows that that tree is there too. If you must hang your food pack, walk deep into the woods and far away from your campsite. And remember, when the food pack is hanging, the aromas are spreading out and around.

A better practice is to lay the food pack in a depression in the ground and cover it with a tarp. For added security, change its location every night. To be extra safe, get yourself bearproof containers.

The best practice is to take your food pack to a nearby island and lay it in a shallow depression.

And keep the MSR cymbals within reach.

A WALK IN THE WOODS

It was too late now, of course, for Sonny to check the general direction that the ATV trail had run. He remembered that Tony had parked the car at the gravel pit at the end of the dirt road and that the ATV trail took off from there, running in a more-or-less straight line for several hundred yards before it seemed to turn, but from where Sonny had been standing at the time, he could not tell in what direction. Had the trail made a sharp turn to the right and continued on in another straight line, he thought that he would eventually reach it, and then it would be a simple matter of following it back to the gravel pit, the car and his friends. He remembered how comfortable he had felt as he walked through the tall grass that separated the gravel pit from the trees, his face being warmed by the mid-afternoon October breeze instead of the sun, which had been hidden behind thick clouds all day long. But that had been about two hours ago.

When they had left the car at about one thirty that afternoon, Sonny and Jim had started walking through the grass to the right of the ATV trail towards the trees, and Tony and John had stayed on the ATV trail. They all had their shotguns ready, and they all were looking forward to several hours of bird hunting. Both pairs of hunters stayed in contact with each other, but as the ATV trail continued on in a straight line, Sonny and Jim had started to veer farther off to the right, and contact between the two pairs became more difficult until it ceased entirely.

By the time Sonny and Jim had reached the tree line, Tony and John had decided to return to the gravel pit and check out another trail that was overgrown and more likely to be hiding partridge. Tony and John turned around and headed back.

When Sonny and Jim reached the tree line, they entered the forest. They hadn't intended to go in too far, but every few steps taken suggested that something more interesting lay just ahead. They came across a decrepit hunting shack, and Jim decided to relieve himself. Sonny continued on a few more steps, but those few steps suggested, as the earlier ones had, that something more would be just ahead. Jim sat down and savored the sweet smell in the warm air as Sonny continued on for a few more steps, and then a few more steps after that. After a minute Jim called to Sonny that he wanted to turn around and go back to the car. Sonny yelled back to Jim that he was going to go on for only a little bit and then turn around and follow him back and that Jim should just go on—he'd be right behind him. Sonny continued on for a bit, but a slight dip led to thicker trees, a gentle turn to the right followed by a sharp turn to the left and before Sonny knew it the path that he had been following had petered out. Sonny turned around and thought he saw the remnants of the path he had been following but he wasn't sure. He decided that it would be easier to head off to the left of the direction he thought he had been walking and bushwhack through the trees until he came to the ATV trail that he remembered had run in a straight line from the gravel pit. He could then follow the trail back towards the car.

He thought that the ATV trail would be close by, certainly within one hundred yards, but after pushing through the branches of the trees for what he thought was long enough, he still hadn't come across the ATV trail. The thickening trees that he had been pushing through suggested no path or game run or trail to follow, and the thickening trees had muffled Sonny's yell to Jim, such that Jim didn't hear Sonny call out. Sonny continued on for a while, continuing to push his way through branches that continued to grab at him and, when they caught him, hold him back. Sonny thought that he saw the trees start to thin and thought that he'd reach the ATV trail momentarily. But what he reached instead was a small clearing in the rough form of a circle, measuring about thirty feet in diameter.

By now Sonny could no longer keep silent the thought that had been growing in the back of his mind that he was, and that he had been for some time, absolutely, unequivocally and most assuredly lost.

"Lost" is a state of being that means different things to different people. To one that does not pay attention, being lost is very simple: not having any idea where one is or how one got there. To one endowed with too much pride, being lost might best be defined as temporarily not knowing exactly where one is at any given moment. A creative person might suggest that being lost means not knowing exactly where one is but at the same time having a good idea about where they are. Of course, the best definition of lost is also the easiest definition: you either know where you are or you don't. There's nothing more to it than that.

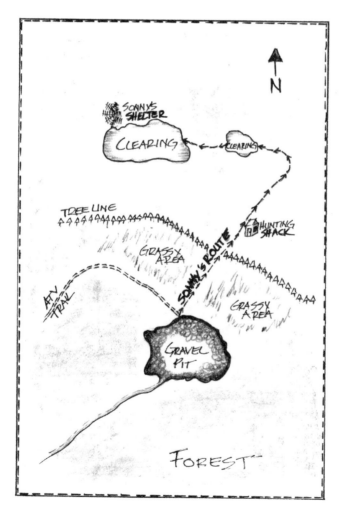

Just as different people have different concepts of what lost means, so do they respond differently when they realize that being lost is what they have become. To a self-assured, confident person, being lost is, at best, a minor inconvenience and, at worst, a minor inconvenience; it's simply a matter of getting back to where they were before they had become lost. To someone who likes a challenge, being lost can stimulate all of one's personal resources. But to Sonny, who was neither confident nor comfortable with challenges, being lost was what it was like for most people: dependent on the circumstances. Being lost in a big city is different from being lost on the highway. Most people have, at one time or another, been lost in a city or on a highway. In both instances the person that is lost knows, and more importantly *believes*, that it's only a matter of time before they figure out where they are, and then it's simply a matter of making up for lost time.

But being lost in the woods entails additional elements that make the experience fundamentally different from being lost anyplace else. The immediately obvious difference is that one is truly alone, without strangers to ask for assistance. The other difference, just as immediate and just as obvious to those brave enough to recognize it, is that being lost in the woods carries with it the possibility of never, ever being found. It's that thought—the possibility that one might never be found, might never get out, might end up as sun-bleached bones picked clean by animals—that makes the experience of being lost in the woods an unforgettable one.

And now it was too late for Sonny to check the general direction that the ATV trail had run. He had a compass with him so he could very easily tell north from south, but without a general reference point, knowing north from south in the woods is not really any better than knowing right from wrong in the woods. Had the sun been out, Sonny would have been able to remember the relationship of the sun in the sky to the ATV trail on the ground and go from there. But the sky had been overcast all day, and all Sonny knew was that, while the sun was behind the clouds, the ATV trail was some place on the ground, and he had absolutely no idea where it was.

Sonny had read some outdoor books, and he had sat with his dad and uncles and listened to them swap stories about deer camp so he knew that, when someone realizes that they are lost in the woods, the first, best thing to do is to simply sit down, take a deep breath, and begin to manage that one thing that if not managed, will surely do one in: one's fear. Sonny remembered that he had, a few times, wondered how he would react to being lost in the woods, and now, at age nineteen with one failing year of college behind him, he was about to find out.

Experienced guides and instructors in outdoor schools have their own guidelines to follow when confronted with a crisis while on the trail. The guidelines are not identical, but they are very similar. It is generally agreed that when confronted with a crisis in the bush the first thing that one must do is establish and maintain a positive mental attitude, and that establishing that all-important positive mental attitude should be done in three seconds. Upon this all depends. Thereafter, a person has about three minutes in which to get oxygen to the brain before suffering irreparable brain damage, which is why an emergency first responder always first checks for a pulse and breathing when coming across an unconscious person. After that the priorities change, depending on one's location and circumstances. If a person is in the woods, they should have a shelter of some type established within three hours. In the short term, shelter is more important than, and paramount to, food and water. A person can survive for up to three days without water and for up to three weeks without food, neither very comfortably, to be sure, and those limits are the outer limits for people who are in good shape and who have been able to establish, and maintain, a positive mental attitude.

But the vast majority of people who die in the woods do not die of thirst or hunger. Rather, they die of what used to be called "exposure" but what is now known as hypothermia. They die because they are wet and cold, and they cannot get dry and warm. They die because their body core temperature drops. One doesn't have to be in the woods in the wintertime to die of hypothermia. Hypothermia doesn't discriminate when it comes to temperature. All hypothermia needs to thrive is a set of conditions—temperature, moisture, wind and physical health—that in combination lower one's body core temperature below a certain level. After that, it's only a matter of time; it becomes a race to raise a person's body core temperature before it sinks to a point where it cannot be raised at all.

The natural progression from drop in body core temperature to a lonely death varies from person to person in terms of time, but not in terms of inevitability. Fit and healthy people die just as inevitably as unfit and unhealthy people—it just takes longer. The first signs of hypothermia are subtle and easily overlooked because they seem so ordinary: fatigue, tiredness, a slight chill. These are easily remedied by rest, food and water and physical activity. Left unattended, however, the signs develop into more dramatic and more apparent symptoms. As a person's body core temperature drops, the body automatically and involuntarily resorts to shivering in an attempt to generate body heat, and in a pathetic attempt to preserve the heat generated, the body will involuntarily raise the hair on legs and arms and back and chest in an attempt to capture and retain that heat next to the skin. If not remedied, more ominous signs develop, most notably behavior that becomes bizarre. It's not uncommon for a rescue squad to find a body of a lost skier in the wintertime only partially clothed; although freezing to death, the hapless skier feels like he is hot and starts to shed clothing in a tragic attempt to cool down. It's ironic that as a person descends into hypothermia they need all of their mental faculties to rescue themselves, yet their mental faculties are impaired, and impaired to the point that the person who needs them doesn't even realize that their mental faculties are fading, and fading fast.

Three seconds for a positive mental attitude, three minutes for oxygen, three hours for shelter, three days for water and three weeks for food were priorities that Sonny had never heard of. He had heard that he should sit down and, while managing his fear, take stock of his situation, whatever it was, and this he did. This is what Sonny found: he was alone, he was nineteen, he was in good health, he had a couple of candy bars in his pockets, he had a compass, he had a shotgun and fifteen shells, he had the clothes on his back, he didn't have any water, he didn't have a map, he had about three hours of daylight left, he didn't have a flashlight, he didn't have any matches or a lighter, he had no idea in which direction he should go, and perhaps most importantly, he did not have any prior experience in being lost in the woods. The things that he didn't have he really didn't think he needed when he and Jim, Tony and John left the gravel pit, hunting for partridge. They had all just had lunch, they were together, it was a warm, pleasant day and they were only going to be gone for a few hours.

But now it was three thirty in the afternoon, and it wasn't quite as warm as it had been. Sonny stood up and pulled out his compass. He found north but that didn't help him at all, because he didn't know where the ATV trail was in relation to north, and he didn't know that because, when he left the gravel pit with his friends a few hours earlier, he hadn't bother to check. Had he checked at the time, he would have learned that the ATV trail ran in a generally southeast/northwest direction. He already knew that the ATV trail had been on his left when he and Jim had walked into the woods. He would have known that all he had to do was find north, and walk to the west, and he could not miss the ATV trail. But all of this was academic, because he didn't know the direction in which the ATV trail ran.

Sonny was presented with a choice. He knew that people would be looking for him, but he didn't know when. He knew that he might have to spend the night in the woods, alone and without a shelter or food, but he also knew that he had about three hours of daylight left. To Sonny, it made more sense to spend the three hours trying to find his way out instead of making preparations for the coming evening. After all, if he found his way out, any time and effort that he had spent in preparing for the evening would have been wasted. This line of reasoning was panic's knock on the door of Sonny's mental calm. Sonny was about to open the door and let panic in. Sonny didn't realize this, of course, for Sonny had already crossed a line that he didn't even know existed. Sonny was thinking, but already Sonny was not thinking clearly.

Panic is terror's little brother. Panic is a taste of what awaits a person that doesn't manage his fear. Panic is a precursor to hysteria. Panic was about to introduce itself to Sonny, and panic's relatives would be along shortly.

Sonny did have the presence of mind to recall all of the road maps that he had looked at. He knew that many roads were laid out along north/south and east/west lines. Maybe, he thought, that ATV trail was also laid out on a north/south or east/west line. If the ATV trail had been laid out on a north/south line, then Sonny would intercept the trail if he walked due west. On the other hand, if the ATV trail had been laid out on an east/west line and Sonny walked west, he'd parallel the ATV trail without realizing it. Sonny looked up at the sky and was heartened to see that the sun was glowing ever so slightly through the thinning overcast, but that really didn't help him, because he hadn't been able to see the sun behind the clouds when he had started out. He could now see the sun but *still* didn't know where the ATV trail was in relation to it.

Sonny had to make a decision. What he should have done, of course, was to stay put and starting collecting the makings of a shelter. What he had already committed to doing, however, was to try and find his way out. He had to decide on a direction. He took a chance and decided that the ATV trail was laid out in a north/south direction, such that if he walked to the west, he would eventually come across it. As it turned out however, and unfortunately for Sonny, the ATV trail wasn't laid out in a north/south direction. The ATV trail ran in a generally southeast/northwest direction before sharply turning south. And when Sonny took a compass reading and started walking through the trees to the west, he started walking roughly parallel to the ATV trail and in doing so stepped deeper into the one-half million acre Kabetogama State Forest.

It would be inaccurate to say that Sonny walked in a westerly direction through the trees. Branches grabbed at him, tugged at his shirt, knocked off his hat, scraped his face and occasionally tripped up his feet; saying that Sonny stumbled in a westerly direction would be more accurate. And his frustrated progress made Sonny even more impatient to get out of the woods. Panic boldly invited itself into Sonny's home when Sonny decided that, the quicker he moved, the more ground he could cover, such that the earlier he'd find the ATV trail. And if he didn't find the ATV trail, if he had hurried he'd have more time to try in another direction. So, Sonny started to push his way through the trees at a faster pace. Panic was now comfortably in Sonny's home, and panic showed no sign of leaving anytime soon.

Sonny pushed on, moving as fast as he could, which wasn't very fast at all because the thick tangle of trees slowed him down. But after awhile the trees started to clear, and Sonny's hopes began to rise. Perhaps the thinning trees suggested that the ATV trail was close by. But even if it wasn't, the thinning trees let Sonny move faster and faster. Soon Sonny found himself in a clearing about two hundred yards long, running as fast as he could. It was as if Sonny was running away from something, which he really wasn't, for the faster that Sonny ran, the faster his pursuers, terror and hysteria, gained on him. It could be said that in this race to overcome panic, terror had caught up with and had snatched the baton from panic's hand. As Sonny neared the end of the clearing he was in full flight, terror in his eyes, in his breathing, and in the stretching of his legs as he desperately tried to go faster, with hysteria closing in just the same.

Sonny was now totally and completely out of control.

And as bad as Sonny's predicament was, it was about to get infinitely worse.

Running as fast as he could through the clearing, Sonny didn't see the nine-inch-tall rock that his right foot barely landed on. Because his right foot barely landed on the rock, his foot slid off to the right, and Sonny rolled his ankle, breaking the fibula, cuboid and the outer metatarsal bones. Sonny fell to the ground, screaming in pain, his ankle broken, his hopes destroyed. He rolled down a slight hill, unable to stop himself, until another hidden rock stopped him—Sonny's head hit the rock and he lay still.

It was four fifteen in the afternoon. A rain squall was about twenty miles to Sonny's west, moving in an easterly direction at about ten miles an hour. The temperature was forty-nine degrees. Sonny was without food, without water, without raingear and without consciousness. Sonny was without hope.

Sonny's travails had not gone unnoticed, for Sonny had been monitored ever since the four friends had left their car, their shotguns at the ready, seeking grouse. Without form, without substance, without a detectable presence of any kind, yet present nevertheless and with a unique intelligence, a dispassionate observer of the future had been watching as Sonny had separated from his friend and become disoriented. The dispassionate observer of the future could not have assisted Sonny even if it had desired to, but this was academic because the dispassionate observer's nature would not recognize caring or sympathy. The dispassionate observer of the future merely watched events unfold as it knew they would. The dispassionate observer of the future observed, without judgment, devoid of inclination to assist. And for what purpose it observed, only it knew.

Sonny awoke to the falling of rain on his face. He had a broken ankle, a minor concussion, and he was wet, cold and hungry. But he was not hysterical, or terrified, or even panicky. He was beyond all of that. Unable to move or shelter himself, he realized the hopelessness of his situation, and he accepted it. He passed a few tears while thinking about his family and how his disappearance would hurt them. He hoped that his body would be found—his family would find some comfort and solace in that. He thought about Megan and wondered how much she would miss him. Romantic relationships are never even or equal; at any given time one partner is more emotionally invested than the other. He had only been out with Megan twice, and he wondered how much she would be affected by his death.

He wondered about his friends and what they had done. Had they gone for help or had they started looking for him on their own? He wondered how long he would survive, exposed and injured. He wondered if he should even try to survive. He wondered how long he could last. The dispassionate observer of the future knew in advance the answers to all of Sonny's wonderings.

Without knowing of anyone in particular, Sonny thought about all of the other people that had become lost in the woods. Without knowing of anyone in particular, he instinctively realized that this kind of thing must happen from time to time. Without knowing of anyone in particular, he instinctively knew that some people found their own way out, that some were found by others, and that some were still missing. He wondered about the apparent randomness of survival and of how little things early on can make big differences later on, such as simply checking the direction of a common ATV trail. He knew that he had exercised bad judgment on this day. And then he recalled one of his uncle's favorite sayings, "In order to have good judgment, you have to survive bad judgment." He thought of his uncle Stan, a combat-wounded veteran from the Vietnam War, and it gave him peace of mind. Sonny was far removed in space and time from that unpopular war, but at this moment he had more in common with his uncle than with anyone else. His uncle had been in desperate circumstances, all alone, wounded and without hope, and he had somehow managed to survive. Sonny thought more of his uncle and he began to pray, not aloud, but from the heart.

Sonny could not walk so he dragged himself by his elbows toward the end of the clearing. The trees were about one hundred feet away, and they offered some shelter. He decided that he would not give up. He decided that he would make his uncle proud of him. He understood that he might still fail and that his uncle would never learn of the heroic measures that his nephew was about to undertake, but Sonny decided then and there that he would live to survive bad judgment. It had taken three hours for Sonny to find his positive mental attitude, and with it, Sonny found hope.

As the dispassionate observer of the future had foreseen, Sonny arrived at the edge of the trees, his elbows bloodied and raw. He dragged himself from spruce tree to spruce tree, breaking off with his hands the branches as high as he could and then, like a beaver, he dragged the branches in his mouth to a particular spruce tree that had unusually low hanging branches. He crawled under the low branches and arranged a wall and a bed of spruce boughs. He was wet, but his little improvised basement tree house would keep him from getting wetter. Proud of his shelter, he relaxed a bit, and he ate one of his two candy bars. And then, from the combined effects of his trauma and his exertions, he passed out and slept.

The dispassionate observer of the future had not been surprised by Sonny's change of attitude and his resilience—it had seen them both coming. The dispassionate observer of the future patiently bided its time and waited for the following days' events to occur.

The next morning brought continuous rain, and Sonny stayed put except for gathering some birch bark from a nearby tree and fashioning a crude container that vaguely resembled a cup. By carefully placing his birch bark cup under the drops of water that dangled from the ends of the needles that he was able to reach, Sonny was able to collect just enough water to drink. He found that his birch bark cup was very inefficient but that it had the virtue of requiring patience, such that he spent the better part of the day crawling on his elbows from pine tree to pine tree, much like a maple syrup farmer periodically taps her trees to harvest sap. By the end of the day his elbows were raw and his ankle was swollen, although not horribly so. For dinner that night he ate his second and last candy bar. And, while he was in extreme pain from his injuries, Sonny was proud that he had lasted the whole day, although he also knew that tomorrow, one way or the other, would be his reckoning day. That tomorrow would be Sonny's reckoning day was also known to the dispassionate observer of the future.

By the evening of this, Sonny's second day, the St. Louis County Rescue Squad had been contacted by Sonny's friends, had mobilized, had set up its headquarters in the gravel pit and had sent several groups out searching for Sonny. The rescue squad had centered on the area around the derelict hunting shack that Sonny and Jim had found on their first day, and it had focused on the north side of the ATV trail on the second day. Tomorrow it would expand its search and include areas farther north and east of the ATV trail.

The morning of the third day found Sonny waking up from his own violent shivering at about ten o'clock. By this time the rescue squad had been in the field for three hours, its members working on very little sleep. Some had been personally involved in a search for a missing hiker on Lake County's Pow Wow Trail several years earlier that had met with success on what surely would have been the last day of that hiker's short life. Yesterday's rain had moved off, and the rescue squad was operating under a blue sky and a bright sun. There were three dozen searchers broken into six different groups, and two of the groups were already searching the area north and east of the ATV trail.

Some time in the afternoon—Sonny was not sure when—he thought he heard a voice. By now his own voice was too weak to yell out, and he was barely able to hoist himself up on to his elbows and look through the side of his makeshift shelter. He was finally able to push himself up. What he saw was the clearing that he had run through, and about one hundred yards away there was a group of six people in uniform. Sonny tried to yell, but his voice made no sound. He knew that he would be saved if he could make some noise, but there was nothing to make any noise with.

That's when Sonny remembered his shotgun. The sound of a shotgun would be all the noise that Sonny needed. But where was his shotgun? Sonny hadn't seen his shotgun all day. In fact, Sonny hadn't even thought about his shotgun since he broke his ankle two days ago. The shotgun, Sonny realized, must be someplace out in the field, lying close to where he had fallen.

Sonny forced himself back up to his elbows and looked out into the field. The pain was unbearable, but the thought of his uncle Stan was stronger. He tried to follow with his eyes the trail he had made when he had dragged himself to the edge of the trees two days earlier. He thought he could see the rock that he had hit his head on. But he couldn't see his shotgun. And then he saw something else: one of the searchers had broken away from the group of six and was walking in his general direction. He was about two hundred feet away from Sonny when he started to slow down. Sonny was two hundred feet away from being rescued and his hopes began to rise.

The dispassionate observer of the future, still monitoring events that it knew would come to pass, had foreseen that one searcher would separate from the main body and start walking in Sonny's direction. The dispassionate observer of the future merely watched Sonny's drama continue to unfold, without emotional investment or empathy and without extending any hope of survival.

The leader of this particular unit of the rescue squad, Lieutenant Patricia McDonnell, was on the radio seeking instructions from her superiors. So far their search had yielded nothing, and she was calling to report that her party was in the middle of a two-hundred-yard-long clearing. Nature being nature, Deputy Deschampe, one of the deputies under her command, had to urinate, and nature being nature, he was not about to do so in front of his female lieutenant, so he excused himself and walked away for some privacy. He was walking directly toward Sonny when he started to slow down.

And this is where timing, luck and random chance introduced themselves to Sonny's drama.

If only the deputy would walk on for another ten feet, he would see something lying on the ground as he tended to Nature's calling. He would recognize what he would see to be a piece of rebar, a length of steel commonly used in the construction industry. He would wonder how it got there. The deputy, who was raised by his parents to revere the Earth, would be offended by what he would see. He would bend down to pick up the piece of rebar with the intent to carry it out and dispose of it properly, but instead of picking up a length of discarded rebar, the deputy would pick up the smooth, polished, black barrel of a Remington model 870 12 gauge shotgun. From a distance of one hundred feet Lieutenant McDonnell would watch her deputy reach down to pick something up. She would think of the young man that they were searching for. She would wonder where he was and if he was still alive.

And three hours later Sonny Laranovich would be in emergency surgery in the Virginia Regional Medical Center, destined to recover, the survivor of bad judgment—if only the deputy walked another ten feet.

So much of life is timing. So much of life is luck. So much of life is random chance. Individually, timing, luck and chance might mean nothing, but collectively they can mean everything. Things happen to one person simply because of the timing, the luck and the random events that happen to another person. Lieutenant McDonnell wasn't even supposed to be in command of this particular search unit on this particular day. Normally Lieutenant Jim Davis would have been in charge. And had he not been injured in a car accident seven days earlier, Lieutenant Davis would have been in the field with Deputy Deschampe.

And with Lieutenant Davis in command, Deputy Deschampe would not have bothered to walk one hundred feet for some privacy to urinate. He would have relieved himself where he stood.

Timing, luck and random chance had placed Lieutenant McDonnell in the field that day as the dispassionate observer of the future knew she would be. Nobody could possibly have recognized the significance a seemingly remote car accident a week earlier would have on Sonny's life, except the dispassionate observer of the future. But here it was, possibly the last act of Sonny's short life about to be played out, and nobody appreciated the significance of Lieutenant McDonnell's presence or of Deputy Deschampe's modesty. Except, of course, the dispassionate observer of the future.

Individually, timing, luck and chance might mean nothing, but collectively they could mean everything to Sonny. The dispassionate observer of the future knew in advance the significance of Deputy Deschampe's departure from the small group of searchers. The dispassionate observer of the future, knowing that Deputy Deschampe would see what appeared to be a piece of rebar if he walked far enough away from Lieutenant McDonnell, would have watched with disinterest as Deputy Deschampe slowed down to stop so that he could relieve himself. The dispassionate observer of the future would have known that if Deputy Deschampe would only walk another ten feet he would see the piece of rebar, reach down to pick it up and grab Sonny's shotgun instead. Sonny's life was hanging in the balance; or to be candid, whether Sonny lived or died would be determined by where Deputy Deschampe stopped. Some people would believe that Sonny was destined to live because Deputy Deschampe was destined to walk that extra ten feet. Other people, people who believe in free will without cosmic interference, would believe that Sonny was destined to die because just where Deputy Deschampe stopped was up to him, period.

Sonny saw the deputy walking toward him. Lieutenant McDonnell saw the deputy walking away from her. The dispassionate observer of the future saw the future unfold. The dispassionate observer of the future saw the deputy start to slow down. The dispassionate observer of the future waited for the future to play out.

In very simple terms, it had come down to this: If Deputy Deschampe walked another ten feet, Sonny would ultimately be saved. If Deputy Deschampe stopped where he was, Sonny was doomed to die of hypothermia in five hours. Sonny's life, and his death, would be determined by, of all things, how comfortable Deputy Deschampe felt as he started to slow down.

And only the dispassionate observer of the future knew what would happen next.

ALTERNATE ENDING TO
A WALK IN THE WOODS
(Sonny's in a World of Hurt)

Author's note: What follows is an alternate ending to "A Walk in the Woods." You'll be able to tell that I had fun writing it. My suggestion is that you not read the alternate ending immediately after reading "A Walk in the Woods" with its original ending. If I have done my job properly, you and your audience will be in no mood to appreciate the alternate ending after listening to Sonny's experiences. Wait a day or so and read the alternate ending around a different campfire.

When we left off, Sonny was is his makeshift shelter, watching a deputy from the rescue squad walking in his general direction because the deputy had to take a leak, and he didn't want to piss in front of his attractive, female lieutenant, the truth be told, he had the hots for.

Sonny's troubles, you will remember, were all of his own making. He had walked into the woods without enough clothes, very little food, no water and without thinking to take a compass reading. In other words, dumb.

Not keeping track of his movements, Sonny had managed to get himself lost, and while running through the woods in a crazed panic, he had tripped, fallen, broken his ankle and knocked himself out. When he came to, he was wet, cold and shivering. He dragged himself to the tree line and built a crude shelter. On the afternoon of his third day in the woods, he heard voices in the clearing that he had fallen in, and he propped himself up on his elbows. He saw a group of people, obvious to him to be a search party. He saw one of the members of the search party walking in his general direction. Sonny was too weak to call out, but maybe it wouldn't matter—if the person kept walking in Sonny's direction, he'd sooner or later step on Sonny. And all of this had been taken in by an extremely bored dispassionate observer of the future.

Continuing on...

Although things were beginning to look up for our boy Sonny, things were about to take a turn for the worse. As in, real worse. For no sooner had the solitary searcher stopped than he immediately disappeared in a flurry of red mist and shredded clothing. Sonny couldn't believe what he had just seen, and what he had just seen made him shiver more violently than his shivering this morning. For there, about two hundred feet away from him, was something that was absolutely, positively and beyond any shadow of a doubt an animal that was supposed to have been extinct for hundreds of millions of years. Yet, there it was, alive and well, having just eaten some lunch and now looking for more—an enormous saber-toothed tiger!

Sonny knew that he could not outrun the ancient cat even if he had been healthy, which he most certainly was not now. He saw the relic feline finish devouring the remainder of the rescue squad and then turn its attention to Sonny. The cat lowered to its haunches, which Sonny knew meant that the dessert-seeking cat was getting ready to pounce. And just as the cat seemed ready to release and cover the two hundred feet between it and Sonny in a single leap, it looked over its left shoulder to see what was making the same noise that Sonny had now just heard.

There, on the far end of the clearing, Sonny saw something only slightly less surprising than the prehistoric cat. It appeared to be a platoon from the Death's Head Division, a particularly nasty and mean-spirited SS division from the World War II—era Wermacht—and one of Hitler's favorites. The platoon was advancing directly onto Sonny's position, and it appeared that there might be a battle between the cat and the Nazi soldiers for the honor and privilege of dispatching Sonny.

The Nazis were about two hundred feet to Sonny's right, with the four-legged eating machine about two hundred feet in front of him.

Sonny wasn't sure if he cared how he checked out. Perhaps he should have cared, for there appeared off to the left a commotion that seemed to have rolled right out of the Bible, and being eaten by the dessert-seeking prehistoric cat or being killed by the Nazis was certainly a better ending than what fate had just dealt Sonny. Yes, you guessed it, there coming out of the trees were none other than the Four Horsemen of the Apocalypse. Who else could one ask for but the original Four Riders? Pestilence, War, Famine and Death. Pestilence riding the white horse, War mounted on the red horse, Famine sitting atop the black horse, and Death upon the pale horse.

Yet even as the Four Horsemen pulled abreast of the saber-toothed tiger and the Nazis, it became apparent that Sonny's troubles had only just begun and that perhaps he had made a mistake in trying to survive. He would have been better off dead, which is how he would surely end if the next visitors, just now arriving, had anything to say about it. Everyone looked up to the sky to witness the arrival, after 654 years at the speed of light from the Gamma Quadrant, of the mothership of the Deltoonians. Hovering a full mile above the forest, the mothership disembarked some of its crew. The Deltoonians were six feet tall and six feet wide with two noses and one eye in each of their two heads. Instead of legs, each Deltoonian had a single wheel that they used to get around, and they maintained their balance with outriggers placed where arms would normally be located.

Their leader pulled out a Montgomery Wards PMP 40-watt professional megaphone and announced to all assembled that they were here to participate in a few alien abductions, and just as soon as they had seized Sonny, they would be on their way. One of the Bible Cowboys (Death, I believe it was, also known as the Grim Reaper) spat on the ground, leveled his scythe and said, "Bite me, you two-headed freak." The saber-toothed tiger growled menacingly, and the Nazis deployed in attack formation.

But even the Deltoonians were not prepared for what, or should I say who, appeared next. Why, it was none other than PMS personified herself: Irene Noumi, Sonny's old fifth grade elementary school teacher. Irene Noumi, all five feet one inch of her, the tormentor of fifth grade students from the old Washington School, the prototype for the Wicked Witch of the West, the one and only Bitch herself, was eyeing Sonny up. She had a yardstick in her hand. Sonny recognized it as the same yardstick that Ms. Noumi had used to whack his knuckles many times before when he had misbehaved in class.

In challenging times it's important for one to retain one's sense of humor, as it may become difficult in the future to keep things in perspective without doing so. So Sonny said aloud to anyone that would listen, "I'm not going to start worrying until the Methhead Gay Bikers for Jesus show up." Just then, Sonny heard the low growl, not of the big cat, but rather of two dozen chopped Harley Davidson motorcycles being driven by good looking guys with crosses around their necks, wearing tight black leather jackets and pants that accentuated their muscular lines and suggested barely controlled power in the homosexual lust department.

Sonny's next thought was, "Oh, crap!" Not because he was frightened by the Methhead Gay Bikers for Jesus, but rather because what happened next. What happened next was that a turkey vulture, having finished digesting last evening's mouse dinner, let out a creamy white poop that fell a few hundred feet before it hit Sonny right square on the face.

Between the saber-toothed tiger, the Nazis, the Four Horsemen of the Apocalypse, the Deltoonians, Irene Noumi, the Methhead Gay Bikers for Jesus and the bird poop on his face, it was looking pretty dicey for our boy Sonny. The animal, the storm troopers, the cowboys from the Bible, the extraterrestrials, the elementary school teacher and the alternative sexual preference motorcycle men, Sonny could handle. But having a bird poop on his face was something that Sonny was beginning to have trouble with.

Sonny decided that enough was enough and that too much was, well, too much. He got up and hobbled into the field, the idea being that whoever wanted him bad enough could have him. As he did so, the Nazis, the Four Horsemen, the Deltoonians, Irene Noumi and the Methhead Gay Bikers for Jesus all formed a circle around Sonny, and all the while they did so, the big cat kept its position, staring Sonny down with its large, black eyes, as its long, sensual, erotic tongue licked its sixteen-inch incisors.

At this point it was anybody's guess as to who would prevail and have Sonny. Each of the contestants boasted a singular quality in its favor. The big cat, for example, brought to the competition unequalled fury. The Nazis prided themselves on being the master race. The Four Horseman were legendary figures that stepped right out of the Old Testament. The Deltoonians boasted unequalled mastery of technology, and Irene Noumi was a witch, pure and simple. The Methhead Gay Bikers for Jesus exuded a strong sense of "Don't you be messing with us, boy."

They all stared at Sonny, who stared back. It was quiet and still, the players being reflective in their moods. Sonny was a goner, the only question remaining to be answered was, "With whom is he going?"

Did I mention the runaway asteroid that was on its way, speeding toward good ol' Mother Earth in general and the Kabetogama State Forest in particular, with its aiming point a perfect bull's-eye formed by a prehistoric cat, a squad of soldiers, four horses with riders, a bunch of aliens, a band of gay bikers and an elementary school teacher, all standing in a circle, and in the middle of the circle, a nineteen-year-old hunter whose face was covered with bird shit?

Meanwhile, the dispassionate observer of the future reached for some more popcorn.

ALWAYS BE SCARED
AND AVOID THE BIG MISTAKES

Ten little boaters letting out their line;
One leaned too far and then there were nine.
Nine little campers liking what they ate;
One lit the campfire and then there were eight.
Eight little hikers thought they were in Heaven;
One climbed a cliff and then there were seven.
Seven little skiers getting in their licks;
One kissed a tree and then there were six.
Six little mushers thrilled to be alive;
One tried the ice and then there were five.
Five little trekkers goin' out for more;
One ate a mushroom and then there were four.
Four little paddlers floating so carefree;
One shot the rapids and then there were three.
Three little hunters stalking in the dew;
One shot a deer and then there were two.
Two little kayakers lookin' for some fun;
One tried the Big Lake and then there was one.
One little trapper trappin' without a gun;
Didn't see the grizzly and then there were none.

Several years ago I had the great privilege of travelling with legendary Registered Maine Guides Garrett and Alexandra Conover in Labrador and Maine. Some years later Garrett spoke at the annual winter camping symposium. Garrett's wise and sage advice, which was meant for wilderness travelers but which also holds true when going about our daily lives, was that we should "always be scared and avoid the big mistakes."

Given the opportunity to elaborate, Garrett recently said, "A person's relationship with the natural world should never be fear stricken or fear driven. Rather, one should always be afraid of assuming too much expertise in uncertain conditions. We should try to keep our mistakes small enough to be survivable, inconvenient enough so that we don't forget the refining lessons and just big enough to keep us humble."

With Garrett's counsel in mind, I wrote the poem, which is based on a similar poem from my childhood.

TRAIL NAMES

People who travel on the trail together should have trail names for one another.

A person's trail name should not be serious; rather, uttering someone's trail name should invoke amusement and mirth among one's companions. "Ridge Runner," for example, is decidedly boring. "Bearpaw O'Reilly," on the other hand, is anything but. One instinctively knows that a tale about "Bearpaw O'Reilly" is bound to be entertaining.

Trail names that ridicule a person's appearance, lack of skill, attitude, aptitude, fancy clothing, high-tech equipment, worn out equipment, poor judgment or prior incidents of incompetence are all fair game and, quite honestly, are preferred.

Trail names should not be bestowed lightly, and a fair amount of thought might be required to generate the appropriate moniker. Once a trail name has been applied, it can be changed, although such modifications require several meetings of the subject's companions (with the subject present, of course), during which the subject's qualities are debated in an attempt to determine if a change is warranted.

Above all, a person cannot christen himself or herself with their own trail name—he or she cannot name themselves. That honor falls to the person's companions, which more or less guarantees amusement and mirth.

Creativity and historical license are both to be encouraged, especially if the trail name is based on the subject's prior episodes of calamity.

Intoxicants have been known to stimulate the imaginations of one's companions, thereby making the hapless soul's trail name particularly hilarious.

SERVE AND VOLLEY

8:00 P.M. ON A THURSDAY EVENING
INSIDE THE STUDIO OF A LOCAL TELEVISION STATION

McConnor: Good evening, ladies and gentlemen, and welcome to this week's edition of *Serve and Volley*. Each week we invite spokespeople from different sides of a contentious issue to debate their case before you, the public. Our rules are simple: our guests all agree to act like adults, they all agree not to interrupt each other and they all promise to afterwards reflect objectively on what their adversary has said. Whether they do so or not is anybody's guess—as you know, we get all kinds of people on this show. When people leave here, we put them on their honor, and we ask them to keep their word. Thanks for joining us. I'm your moderator, Jack McConnor. Tonight's subject: The Boundary Waters Canoe Area Wilderness: Living Within the Rules. Joining us this evening are Emily Wilson and Scott Blue. Ms. Wilson appears on behalf of a coalition of groups dedicated to keeping the Boundary Waters open to everybody and for all uses. Scott Blue appears on behalf of a separate coalition of environmental groups that collectively strives to preserve the Boundary Waters in its present state by limiting the number of people that use the Boundary Waters and by also restricting certain activities. Mr. Blue—let's start with you. Living within the rules—why should we?

Blue: Are you serious?

McConnor: Yeah, I'm serious. Why should people follow regulations that the Forest Service enacts when the Forest Service itself doesn't follow its own regulations?

Blue: Maybe if you could give me an example of...

McConnor: The last time I was in the Boundary Waters I was walking on boardwalk that the Forest Service installed on a very muddy part of a portage. How do you square the use of boardwalk with the Forest Service's catchy little hook of "leave no trace"?

Blue: Talk about not following one's own rules. You began by telling the audience that there would be no interruptions, yet you interrupted me when I began to answer your question. Should I expect more of the same or are you going to let me talk?

McConnor: Answer the question, please.

Blue: Again, should I expect more of the...

McConnor: I said answer the question.

Blue: (momentarily pausing) Boardwalk is used in isolated areas to control erosion and limit damage to the portages. If people want to go someplace bad enough, they'll get there one way or the other. So, it's better to use boardwalk or corduroy or some other similar technique than to just do nothing and let people rip up the portages.

McConnor: That's a convenient answer, but it also ignores the larger hypocrisy that I see: official campsites with cast iron fire grates and fiberglass toilets. Every time I'm in the Boundary Waters I see evidence of the Forest Service telling me where I have to camp, where I have to build a fire and where I have to take a dump. All of these visible signs from an agency that tells me to leave no trace. What gives?

Blue: Again, the idea is to see that people use the wilderness in such a way that it is not permanently damaged. Telling people where they can camp is not a tremendous inconvenience to them. The sites are appropriately placed. The use of fiberglass toilets concentrates the waste to a given area. When you think about it, do you really want to have people leaving stools all over a campsite? As for the fire grates—that's a nonissue, and I'm surprised that you even brought it up. Fire grates, when properly used, contain fires.

Without that containment the risk of a small campfire getting out of control increases astronomically. It sounds to me like you are advocating no controls at all. What do you want? Half of the campsites in the Boundary Waters reduced to ashes and the other half covered with dung?

McConnor: I'm trying to address the hypocrisy here. Why the motto? Why tell people to leave no trace? You can't have it both ways. Either the Forest Service itself leaves no trace or it should stop telling the campers to leave no trace.

Blue: I can't speak for the Forest Service but I can say...

Wilson: What do you mean you can't speak for the Forest Service? From the way you've been talking it sounds to me like you're on their payroll!

Blue: Mr. McConnor, should I wait for you to tell Ms. Wilson not to interrupt me or should I do it myself?

McConnor: I'm the one who decides what passes for...

Blue: (interrupting) Passes for what? Entertainment? Dissemination of misinformation? What exactly do you pass on?

McConnor: Get back to the point, Mr. Blue—the point that Ms. Wilson has nailed you with. Sounds to me like you're an apologist for the Forest Service.

Blue: If you want the official Forest Service position, then you should get a representative of the Forest Service here. If you want my opinion, which I guess you do, because you *did* invite me here, I'll give it to you.

McConnor: Would you agree that the Forest Service's position is that the number of people and what those people do have to be regulated?

Wilson: Here it comes...some more words that...

McConnor: (to Wilson) Be quiet. Let him talk.

Blue: We're just asking the people who use the wilderness to leave it in the same condition that they found it. That's all. Because once a wilderness is gone, it really is gone forever.

McConnor: And you still haven't answered my question: why the motto if the Forest Service doesn't practice what it preaches?

Wilson: You're not going to get an answer from him because he has no answer to give you. This is just an example of government hypocrisy—unelected government officials telling us how to live but not following their own rules. Typical liberal.

McConnor: I just told you to be quiet, now I'm telling you to shut up!

Blue: This has nothing to do with politics.

Wilson: It's got nothing to do with common sense either. There are no designated campsites in the Quetico, there are no cast iron fire grates in the Quetico and there are no fiberglass toilets there either. They seem to get along pretty well up there.

Blue: Different circumstances entirely. Substantially fewer people. More remote. You're comparing apples and oranges.

Wilson: What about dogs? Dogs are pooping in the Boundary Waters throughout the year. What's next? Is your coalition of elitists going to want wild animals to use toilets too? Or is it just domesticated pets that will have to pick up after themselves?

Blue: Don't be silly.

Wilson: I'm not being silly. I'm being serious. The Forest Service has imposed regulations that limit the use of public areas to a select, chosen few. If you're not a person who likes to paddle a canoe, you're just out of luck.

Blue: What do you mean by a select, chosen few? There is no litmus test that a camper has to take before they enter the wilderness. We don't care who enters the wilderness, as long as they respect the law.

Wilson: An enormous area of public land has been set aside for the use of only a few—those few that paddle canoes. And in the winter it's even worse—nobody is paddling a canoe in the Boundary Waters in the winter. I bet that on any given night in the winter there aren't a hundred people camping in the Boundary Waters either. Yet there are thousands of snowmobilers that would like to travel that country, but they're not allowed to because we don't want to disturb less than a hundred campers? C'mon—give me a break!

Blue: Restricting snowmobiles has nothing to do with saving the Boundary Waters for wintertime campers. It's all about trying to preserve a last, little bit of wilderness.

McConnor: How about it, Ms. Wilson? What's wrong with designating a specific area and telling people "no motors and no noise"?

Wilson: Thousands of taxpayers are denied the…

Blue: My tax dollars are spent to keep up snowmobile trails throughout this state. I don't complain about that.

McConnor: Ms. Wilson, do you support the completely unrestricted use of the Boundary Waters by as many people that can get there by any means possible?

Wilson: I support opening up the Boundary Waters so that taxpaying citizens can use it.

McConnor: Now you're the one who's not answering questions. Answer me, and right now. Do you advocate the completely unrestricted use of the Boundary Waters by as many people that can get there by any means possible? It's not a trick question, Ms. Wilson. It's easily answered with a yes or a no. What's your answer?

Wilson: We need to open the area up so that more people can use it the way they want to use it.

McConnor: And what about the effect on the area. Whether you like it or not, Mr. Blue over here is correct when he says that once a wilderness is gone, it's gone.

Wilson: I have a neighbor. He's a combat-wounded veteran who served our country. He can't carry a canoe anymore because of his war-related injuries. Do you want to keep him out of the Boundary Waters?

McConnor: I ask the questions here, Ms. Wilson.

Wilson: Why don't you ask Mr. Forest Service Agent if it's fair that a combat-wounded veteran can't use the Boundary Waters?

Blue: The reason that we believe that…

McConnor: (to Blue) What about this rule limiting the number of people in any one place to nine? What's magical about nine? Why not seven, or ten?

Blue: The BW is a fragile ecosystem that can be easily upended, with disastrous consequences for all who use it.

McConnor: I see another conflict within your regulations. What happens when there is one campsite on a lake and it's already occupied by seven campers. My group is looking for a place to camp, and there are four of us. It's late in the day, and we need a place to camp. What do we do? Do we join the group of seven, which brings the total to eleven, or do we make our own campsite?

Blue: You should have started out earlier.

McConnor: Whaddya mean, we should have started out earlier? We started out on time, but we were delayed. There was a thunderstorm. There was a windstorm. One of our party blew out his knee on a portage and that slowed us up. We got a late start because the person who gave us our permit couldn't get the video to play, and bureaucrat that she was, she wouldn't give us our permit until we had watched the video. We were delayed for an hour and a half. There's any number of reasons why someone might be looking for a campsite late in the day. The real reason why a party might not be able to find a campsite is that there aren't enough campsites. What do those people do? Do they join another group, or do they make their own unofficial site or do they...?

Wilson: Good point.

McConnor: I told you to be quiet, I told you to shut up and now I'm telling you to shut your God da...

Blue: It's not a good point. It's a red herring, is what it is. Rules and regulations should not be singled out with unlikely scenarios in mind, but rather with likely, everyday scenarios in mind.

McConnor: I want an answer to my question.

Blue: If you'd be quiet for a minute I'd give you one. Could someone receive a citation for camping where they should not? Of course they could. But would they? It's difficult for me to imagine someone being cited for setting up a camp when they had no other choice. The Forest Service relies on the judgment of its people in the field. If bad weather or an injury caused someone to set up a camp where they should not have, they're not going to get cited. I know that the pro-use groups like Ms. Wilson's don't like to acknowledge that the Forest Service people are human, but they are.

Wilson: Actually, for humans, I think they're pretty cold. Those rules and regulations are made up and passed by people who we don't know and who don't live here and who don't have to answer to the people who *do* live here.

Blue: They're not cold at all. The problem you have with them is that they pass rules and regulations that you don't like. And because you don't like the rules and regulations, then you don't like the people who adopted them, and especially the people who enforce them. That's a real mature attitude there, Ms. Wilson. Why don't you take your snowmobile and go home?

McConnor: (to Wilson) Are you gonna take that crap from him?

Wilson: (to Blue) Listen to me, you bald-headed old fart...

Blue: Not too mature there, Emily. Graduate from elementary school yet? I doubt it.

Wilson: What about the people across the street from me? They're an older couple. He walks with a cane, and she needs a walker. I guess their Boundary Waters days are over because they can't get over the first portage.

McConnor: Seems to me like lots of people want to go to the Boundary Waters but they don't, either because they can't get a permit or because they can't use a motor.

Blue: Legally, everyone can use the wilderness, but the wilderness is not for everyone. There are many people who physically can't put up with the rigors of wilderness travel.

Those people shouldn't be in the wilderness. Just like the mountains aren't for everyone. There are countless people who would like to be hiking in the mountains but can't because of their health. Are you suggesting that we build stairways and escalators and install powered lifts so that people with handicaps can watch the sun set behind some snow-covered peak?

McConnor: But why does it have to be a wilderness in the first place? What's so special about that? Seems to me that you're making a value judgment here—protect the land for the animals instead of letting the humans use the land.

Blue: You two seem to be reading from the same page. Are the two of you stopping for a drink after the show?

McConnor: Why preserve the land for the animals instead of letting the people use the land? That land *is* owned by the people, by the way. The people that own the land need a permit to use the land? What sense does that make?

Blue: What the coalition that I speak for is trying to do is keep the Boundary Waters in its natural state so that we…

Wilson: Natural state? Natural state? What are you talking about? Do you know anything about the history of the Boundary Waters?

Blue: As a matter of fact, I do.

Wilson: As a matter of fact, you don't! What you see when you go into the Boundary Waters today is not the Boundary Waters in its natural state. The Boundary Waters today looks completely different from what it looked like a hundred years ago. You're not the least bit interested in preserving the Boundary Waters in its natural state. You're just trying to preserve the Boundary Waters in a state that you like. There is no natural state of the Boundary Waters. The Boundary Waters has always been changing. It won't look the same way a hundred years from now as it looks today.

Blue: Well, not if you have anything to do with it. You'd like nothing better than to get boats and motors and snowmobiles into the middle of the only canoe wilderness left in the United States.

Wilson: The Boundary Waters should be open for use by all. Not just for a few privileged elite.

McConnor: What do you mean, a few privileged elite? Take a good look at the people going in and coming out. They don't look very privileged to me. And elitist? Check out the parking lot at Sawbill and tell me how many pickup trucks are there, and then tell me if there's a single Lexus anywhere to be seen. Go ahead.

Wilson: Poor choice of words on my part. What I'm trying to say is that the government has taken this large area—over one million acres in size—and basically said, stay out unless you...

McConnor: That's the whole point! People with big motors and snow machines have lots of lakes and trails to play on with their noisy toys. What's wrong with saying you can have your big boat and your big motor, but go play with it across the street. Or better yet, take your loud, obnoxious toy and play with it where I don't have to listen to it. What's next? I suppose you want to be able to walk into a restaurant and start smoking.

Wilson: Talk about red herrings! Smoking in restaurants has nothing to do with...

McConnor: Of course it does! You're a libertine, Ms. Wilson. You want to be able to do anything, anyplace at any time, and you don't like it when someone says you can't. You don't give a hoot about what happens to one of the last remaining wilderness areas in our country, just as long as you can use it the way you want to use it.

Wilson: Countless people have been put out of work and have been forced to move away to find jobs, because they couldn't do the job that they wanted to do here. Guiding, for example.

McConnor: Hard for me to believe that countless people, as you describe the number, have moved to Tennessee or Arkansas because they could no longer guide in the Boundary Waters.

Wilson: The government has taken this million-acre tract of land out of public use.

Blue: By bandying around the number one million you make it sound like it's a huge tract of land. It's not. Want to know just how small one million acres is? Just open up your highway map of Minnesota, take a step back and take a good look. You'll see that the area that we're talking about, while it sounds extremely large, really isn't that big at all when compared with the size of the state.

Wilson: I want to change the subject here for a minute and get back...

McConnor: We're not changing the subject because I like the subject that we're on right now.

Wilson: The point that I want to make is that...

McConnor: I don't care what point you want to make. Shut your pie hole or I'll tape it shut. Maybe you'd lose some weight.

Wilson: I want to...

McConnor: I don't care what you want to do. What you should do is not let Mr. Green here or Mr. Orange or Mr. Purple push you around. Can't you do any better than how you're doing?

Wilson: I'm trying to...

McConnor: You're trying to ignore the fact that you're embarrassing yourself. And as for you, Mr. Rainbow...

Blue: (grimacing, and with a threatening tone in his voice) Yes?

McConnor: Weak, pretty weak. You're what we in the industry call a cream puff.

Blue: Cream puff?

McConnor: Soft in the middle.

Blue: I think you need to be quiet so that I can talk.

McConnor: Maybe you think you can make me be quiet?

Wilson: He's a coward. You'll never get him to...

McConnor: Talk about a coward. You're the one hiding behind your skirt.

Wilson: It's the...

McConnor: What did you do before you became a mouthpiece for the snowmobile industry?

Wilson: Listen here. If you think that you can...

McConnor: I think that maybe you should try to shut Mr. Blue here up. Why don't you get up close and personal with him during the break? Or is it because you're afraid of him?

Wilson: This is crazy.

Blue: Well, there's at least one thing that we agree on.

McConnor: Actually, Mr. Blue, you're the one hiding behind the skirt.

Blue: (standing up) It's time that someone showed you some manners.

McConnor: (standing up) Like you? Certainly little Miss Priss here won't.

Wilson: (standing up and approaching McConnor) Hey, Jack...

McConnor: What?

Wilson: (taking a swing and connecting) Want another one?

Blue: Hey, Jack...

McConnor: (bleeding from his lower lip) What?

Blue: (taking a swing and connecting) Here's another one.

McConnor: (bleeding from the lower lip and nose): You little shi...

Wilson: Why are you calling him names? I'm the one who hit you first. I don't like being ignored. (swinging again) Here—have another one.

Blue: Hey Jack, you're getting beat up by a girl.

Wilson: (approaching Blue) Who in the hell are you calling a girl?

Blue: (approaching Wilson) My mistake. I'm so terribly sorry. You're not a girl. You're a pampered, spoiled little slu...

Producer: (to technical assistant off stage) Call 911 and get the cops here. Jack's got some people wound up again.

MONDAY MORNING, THREE DAYS LATER 11:50 A.M.
ARRAIGNMENT COURTROOM, FIRST FLOOR
ST. LOUIS COUNTY COURTHOUSE
DULUTH, MINNESOTA

Judge: We're running out of time Esther—it's almost noon. Anyone still left in lockup?

Esther: We still have to arraign those three *Serve and Volley* people.

Judge: Oh yeah. I forgot. Well, better get 'em in here. I'm getting hungry.

Esther: (on telephone to holding cell area) Bring in McConnor, Wilson and Blue.

Judge: (chuckling) *Serve and Volley* people...more disorderly conducts?

Esther: No. Things got carried away this time. (on telephone to holding cell) The judge said to bring in all three...I don't care if he doesn't want to come...I don't care...(whispering)...look, His Holiness is hungry so get him in here. If he's not in here by the time I put the phone down I'm gonna send Leo in there with his cattle prod.

Judge: Something going on in lockup?

Esther: McConnor doesn't want to come.

Judge: McConnor, eh? Well, I don't blame him. He'll remember me from the last time he was here.

TWO MINUTES LATER
THE JAILER ESCORTS THREE PRISONERS
INTO THE COURTROOM

Jailer: Mr. Blue, just have a seat in the front row. Ms. Wilson, take a seat in the back row, please. Mr. McConnor, front row. And don't forget, I've got more where that came from, in case you haven't had enough.

Judge: What's that smell?

Jailer: Chemical irritant, your honor.

Judge: From where?

Jailer: Mr. McConnor was getting feisty. I had to hose him down.

Judge: Oh, OK. Esther.

Esther: Number 23 on the second docket. State of Minnesota vs. Emily Wilson.

Judge: You are Emily Wilson?

Wilson: Yes, Your Honor.

Judge: What's your address please?

Wilson: 423 Lake Trail, Thomas, Minnesota.

Judge: Ms. Wilson, you're appearing today on a misdemeanor level offense of fifth degree assault. Do you understand the charge?

Wilson: Yes, Your Honor.

Judge: Do you understand your rights?

Wilson: Yes, Your Honor.

Judge: Are you ready to enter a plea today?

Wilson: Not guilty, Your Honor.

Judge: OK, we'll give you a date for your next hearing. Esther?

Esther: Pretrial conference on October 6 at ten o'clock.

Judge: You understand that, Ms. Wilson?

Wilson: Yes, Your Honor.

Judge: That's three weeks away. What should I do with you until then?

Wilson: I'd like to be released. I don't have a prior record.

Judge: What about that matter from three years ago when you were fined for operating your snow machine in a prohibited area?

Wilson: That was supposed to be dropped if I behaved myself.

Judge: If these reports are true, you have not behaved yourself, Ms. Wilson.

Wilson: Your Honor, I have…

Judge: Ever fail to appear for a court hearing before, Ms. Wilson?

Wilson: No, Your Honor.

Judge:	Well, Ms. Wilson, I'm going to ROR you.
Wilson:	ROR?
Judge:	Release you on your own recognizance. But you have to promise me that you're not going to have any contact with Mr. Blue or Mr. McConnor. Understood?
Wilson:	Yes, Your Honor.
Judge:	Be back here on October 6 at ten o'clock.
Wilson:	Yes, Your Honor.
Judge:	OK, just have a seat. Esther?
Esther:	Number 24 on the second docket. State of Minnesota vs. Scott Blue.
Judge:	Are you Mr. Blue?
Blue:	Yes, Your Honor.
Judge:	And your address?
Blue:	78 Court Street, Leslie, Minnesota.
Judge:	Where's Leslie?
Blue:	Southwest part of the state, Your Honor.
Judge:	Mr. Blue, do you understand why you're here today?
Blue:	Fifth degree assault, Your Honor.
Judge:	Do you understand your rights?
Blue:	Yes, Your Honor.
Judge:	Do you know what you want to do today, Mr. Blue?
Blue:	Not guilty, Your Honor.
Judge:	Esther?
Esther:	Pretrial conference on October 8 at ten o'clock.
Judge:	Mr. Blue, we're giving you a date for your next court hearing different from that of Ms. Wilson's. What should I do with you in the meantime?
Blue:	I don't have a prior record, Your Honor. Certainly no convictions for illegally operating a snow machine in a prohibited area like Ms. Wilson has.
Judge:	I'm tempted to release you on ROR, Mr. Blue, but another comment like that and I'm going to be even more tempt-

ed to have our friendly sheriff feed, clothe and house you
until your next hearing. Interested in that, are you, sir?

Blue: No, Your Honor. I'm sorry, Your Honor.

Judge: What happened to your eye?

Blue: I got sucker punched by that bit...

Judge: Yes? You were going to say something more?

Blue: (thinking) Nothing, Your Honor.

Judge: Wise decision on your part. Mr. Blue, I'm going to turn
            you loose. Be back for court on October 8 at ten o'clock,
            and stay away from Ms. Wilson and Mr. McConnor.

Blue: Yes, Your Honor.

Judge: Esther?

Esther: Number 25 on the second docket. State of Minnesota vs.
            Jack McConnor.

Judge: Welcome back, Mr. McConnor. Hasn't been all that long
            since we saw you last. Been well, have you?

McConnor: Your Honor.

Judge: Mr. McConnor, you're appearing today on the felony-level
            offense of inciting a riot.

McConnor: I want a different judge.

Judge: No one else is available at the moment. Here are your
            choices: either I arraign you or you'll have to wait until
            we find another judge to arraign you.

McConnor: How long is that going to take?

Judge: I don't know.

McConner: (mulling his options over) I didn't incite a...

Judge: Mr. McConnor, we're not here today to decide guilt or
            innocence. All we're doing today is giving you another
            court date and deciding what to do with you until then.

McConnor: I want to be released.

Judge: Everybody always wants to be released.

McConnor: But I deserve to be released.

Judge: This being a felony-level offense, we're going to be sched-
            uling an omnibus hearing for you. Esther?

Esther: September 23 at one thirty.

Judge: Mr. McConnor, your next hearing is going to be on September 23 at one thirty. Because it's a felony-level offense...

McConnor: How can what I did be a felony? It's overcharged!

Judge: You sound like a defense attorney.

McConnor: Your Honor, I'm going to...

Judge: I'm going to set bail in the amount of ten thousand dollars and refer you to supervised release. Maybe they'll take you. That's all.

McConnor: I'll just...

Judge: (to the jailer) You can take them back to lockup. Mr. Blue and Ms. Wilson can be released. You can hold Mr. McConnor until he either bails or SR takes him.

TWO MINUTES LATER, AND AFTER
THE JAILER HAS ESCORTED THE
THREE PRISONERS OUT OF THE COURTROOM

Esther: That was a long morning.

Judge: Yeah, it was.

Esther: I'll see you after lunch.

Judge: OK. Oh, by the way, Esther, I have a question.

Esther: Yes?

Judge: How long have you been calling me "His Holiness" behind my back?

Esther: (looking directly at the judge) Ever since you started walking on the water, Your Honor.

WHY CAN'T WE ALL JUST GET ALONG?

I was paddling down the Little Isabella River not all that long ago, doing yet another "connecting the dots" trip on my map, in this case, the dots being Quadga Lake to the east and Bald Eagle Lake to the west. There was a six-mile stretch at the end of the Isabella River that I had not yet explored. The Little Isabella dumps into the bigger Isabella a good mile west of Quadga, and my plan was to paddle down the little river to the bigger river, take a slight detour to the east to Quadga, and then turn around and continue west, down the Isabella, to Bald Eagle Lake. Nature had conveniently located the Snake River at the southern tip of Bald Eagle Lake, and by paddling up the Snake, I could reach a landing that was close to a gravel road only about two miles from my car, and I could easily walk that. A nice little loop, comfortably done in the four days that I had set aside, and I'd even have some time to do some sightseeing on Bald Eagle Lake if I wanted.

This was a solo trip. The Outdoors writer of the local newspaper claimed once to occasionally be accompanied on his solo trips by his imaginary friend, one "Blueberry Hanson." I didn't feel like travelling alone, but I didn't feel it would be appropriate to ask if I could borrow Blueberry for a few days, so I brought along my buddies, named Me and Myself. Me, Myself and I get along famously—probably because they always agree with what I want to do. And after all, it *is* always about yours truly. So Me, Myself and I climbed into my solo Dagger canoe and set off on another Boundary Waters adventure. My companions don't take up much room, they don't eat anything at all and I'd at least have someone to talk to. Both of them listen well.

The third night found me camped at a site on the southern end of Bald Eagle Lake. It had been a good trip, and I was able to get up to Quadga, paddle down the Isabella River and explore Bald Eagle.

Tomorrow I'd pack up, round up my companions and paddle out of the wilderness and back to civilization. And to other living people. My buddies were getting boring.

With the memory of last year's Lake Polly Bear still fresh in my mind, I made it a point to protect my food by moving my stash around every night. So far I had not had any problems. After dinner I cleaned the dishes, collected some more firewood and then turned to the task of hiding my food from nosy and hungry critters of all shapes and sizes. All of the food went into a plastic bag, which went into a dry bag and then I trudged off a hundred yards from my campsite where I found a slight depression in the ground about twenty feet from a flat rock behind a dead birch tree. I put the dry bag down, covered it with some leaves and then returned to my campsite to build a fire, relax and enjoy the evening by having a few refreshments (I always travel with some of my favorite bourbon—the one and only Jim Beam.)

I took a sip of Beam from my Nalgene bottle, and a few minutes later, I took another sip. I thought about what trip I would do next, and to lubricate my thinking, I took a few more sips. I asked my silent companions if they wanted any bourbon, but they remained characteristically quiet. "All the more for me to enjoy," I thought as I smiled before another sip. An unseen loon called out with its haunting wail, and now operating under the effect of several sips of bourbon, I wailed back. "A pretty good imitation," I said to myself, prior to taking another sip. I thought that my second wail was even better than my first.

After awhile my mood and my Nalgene bottle had both become noticeably lighter, and I made a mental note to increase my allotment of Jim Beam on future trips—a litre just doesn't go as far as it used to. But I was feeling quite mellow as it was, and I certainly was not about to raid my first aid kit for one of those little white pills that my primary care physician had prescribed for me, the possession of which without a valid prescription is a felony-level offense.

The crackling of the fire seduced my ears, while the wispy blue smoke drifted about and the cool air caressed my cheeks. The deepening sunset seemed to dance in the many drops of dew on the sitting log. It was a perfect Boundary Waters evening to enjoy. And then

I suddenly realized that I was not enjoying the evening alone, for my campfire was being reflected by two little eyes fronting a massive form not thirty feet away from me. What appeared to be a large, dark bush raised its snout, took a few sniffs, mulled things over and decided to approach. And there I was again, for the second time in as many years, face-to-face with a big, black bear.

The bear slowly sauntered up and, standing on all fours on the other side of the campfire, looked at me intently. I looked back—there was nothing much else I could do, and my travelling buddies were nowhere to be seen. The bear looked down at the sitting log at his feet, looked up at me again, looked down at the log again and then, without raising its head but moving its eyes until they met mine, said to me, "Do you mind if I sit down?"

I was speechless.

What seemed like a week passed before I was able to think straight, and the bourbon wasn't helping matters. Regardless of the unbelievable events that had just presented themselves to me, I decided that proper etiquette required a response—anything else would have been rude. So I replied, "Why, no. Have a seat."

The bear stepped over the sitting log and then leaned back, placed his substantial rump on the sitting log and sat down with a heavy thud. The sitting log seemed to groan under its weight. This was a big bear. The bear sat up straight, just like I was, and his back feet were flat on the ground, just like mine were. With his right front paw he motioned to my almost empty Nalgene bottle lying on the ground and said, "Have any more of that?"

"What? This?" I questioned. "You want some of my Jim Beam?"

"If you don't mind," answered the bear.

Keeping my eyes fixed on this wild beast that had somehow achieved human speech, I reached down and fumbled around for a bit until I felt the Nalgene bottle. I picked it up and cautiously leaned forward, stretched out my left hand, offered the bottle to the bear and said, "Help yourself, but that's all I have left."

The bear looked at me and said, "You'll have to take the cap off. I don't have opposable thumbs, ya know."

Feeling somewhat embarrassed by my insensitivity to the creature's dilemma, I removed the cap and handed the bottle back to the bear.

The bear lifted the bottle with both front paws, tilted its head back and, before tipping the bottle, said to me, "Don't worry, I won't drink too much."

The bear emptied the bottle in a single gulp and let out a moderately loud burp. And then the bear stuck his tongue into the Nalgene bottle and licked it dry. It was the longest tongue I had ever seen. It looked like it was twice as long as the tongue that the butcher sells.

The bear dropped the bottle to the ground and, after a long moment, said to me, "Let's talk," followed by another burp.

"Okay," I replied, still not knowing what else to do. "About what?"

"It doesn't have to be this way, ya know," said the bear.

"What way is that?" I asked.

"I saw you hiding your food back up there in the woods," the bear claimed. "I thought about digging it up and ripping the bag open. It wouldn't be hard to do. But there has to be a better way."

"What way are you talking about?" I asked the bear. Aside from being amazed, I was also a bit confused by what the bear was leading up to.

"About me eating," said the bear. "You can only eat so many blueberries, ya know. After awhile, you get sick of eating blueberries. Try it."

"Well," I said as I surveyed the bear, "you seem to be eating all right. Looks to me like you're a charter member of the clean plate club."

"Sometimes I find a bees' nest and I eat a bunch of honey. But I pay for it big time. Those little buggers bite fast and quick. And there's lots of them. But usually it's just nuts and fish guts and insects. And blueberries."

"What are you suggesting?" I asked the bear.

The bear replied, "Well, it seems to me like we should be able to work out some sort of accommodation. The way things are now, when I find a food pack I eat everything inside. I've sent a lot of canoe campers back home early with shredded packs because they didn't have any food left. I get my fill, and you campers get pissed at me. You have to leave early, and you have to replace your packs. But sometimes

I can't find a food pack, and I end up eating nuts and fish guts and insects. And sometimes some honey. And those damn blueberries."

"And what am I supposed to do about that?" I countered.

The bear paused a long time before carefully answering. "Well," said the bear, "if you would leave some of your food out in the open, I'd agree to eat only what you'd leave, and I wouldn't touch any of the other food in your food packs."

"You want me to leave food out for you on purpose?" I was shocked.

"Yeah," answered the bear. "I get to eat some different food, and you don't lose all of your food. You don't have to leave early. And you don't have to replace your food packs. Works for both sides."

"What do you mean, both sides? Are you telling me that you represent a passel of bears? What, have you guys unionized? Are you a bear lawyer or something? Are you affiliated with the Teamsters?"

"Don't be silly," replied the bear. "All I'm saying is that there are several of us in this area that would agree to not raid your food packs. All we want is something for our good behavior."

"This sounds like a shakedown," I protested. "What, are you from Chicago? I guess I know why they're called the Chicago Bears."

The bear gave a slight smile and tauntingly said, "I understand that you met my cousin last year."

"What do you mean I met your cousin last year?" I asked.

"Black Bart told me that he raided your campsite on Lake Polly."

I was startled, and it took some time for me to regain my composure. When I had recovered, I asked the bear, "You mean to say that you guys have names?"

"Of course we have names," answered the bear.

"What's your name?" I asked the bear.

"You couldn't pronounce it," replied the bear.

"And you talk to each other?" I asked.

"Don't you talk to your relatives?" The bear answered my question with one of his own. Before I could respond, the bear continued. "I had a distant cousin named Jumpy Jake in northwestern Montana. Nine hundred pounds. Big animal. Brown, silver tipped coat and a dished-in face. Six-inch claws. He got tired of eating berries, so he started eating people, but he quit after he ate a lawyer. He didn't like the taste that the lawyer left in his mouth," the bear explained wryly.

So, I thought, not only had this bear achieved speech, but he had developed an appreciation for humor as well.

"But," continued the bear, "they finally got around to shooting ol' Jake. He's on display someplace in Missoula. Big animal."

"You want me to purposely leave food out so that you can eat it? This is insane. It kind of reminds me of that suggestion to legalize marijuana," I said. "Legalize drugs and reduce crime. That never gets anyplace."

"I'm not talking about drugs," said the bear. "I just want some different food to eat. That's all."

"And if I say no? Then what?"

"Well," said the bear, "I know that your dry bag is buried under those leaves twenty feet from the flat rock behind the dead birch tree. I'll be having a late night snack tonight, and you won't be having any breakfast tomorrow."

"This is a bit much for me. I have to think this over. Maybe see my psychiatrist while I'm at it," I said wearily.

"Take all the time you need," said the bear. "But I'm hungry right now."

The bear and I stared at each other.

The bear got up, turned and stepped over the log it had been sitting on. He waddled back toward the forest from where he had come, but just before reaching the dense brush he turned to me and said, "Jim Beam is fine, but Barclay's is better. Too bad Barclay's was discontinued last year." He turned and slowly stepped into the forest, melded with the brush and faded away.

I awoke to the mid-morning sun warming my cheek. I had spent the night curled around the fire grate. A chipmunk was gnawing on a bit of yesterday's dinner not five feet away from me. The look on his face suggested that he had been awake for many hours; the look on his face also questioned why hadn't I been, too. My head was throbbing, and I sat up slowly and tried to remember what had happened. All I could recall was that, after the bear had left, I stood up, not knowing what I was supposed to do, or if I should do anything at all. I remembered taking a few steps and then starting to feel dizzy. I remembered trying to sit back down, but I must have lost my balance and fell over and hit my head on the fire grate.

"Strange dream," I said to Me, and Myself. As usual, we all agreed.

I was hungry, so I went up to get the food bag. I walked into the woods and found the flat rock behind the dead birch tree. Twenty feet away was a small pile of leaves. I brushed the leaves aside, and to my surprise, my dry bag with my food was gone. In its place was an empty Nalgene bottle.

I paddled out without having any breakfast, not knowing if I should quit doing solo trips, or if I should quit drinking, or if I should quit both.

Or maybe next time I should just leave some food out in the open and hope for the best.

FOREVER YOUNG

A good friend and I were backpacking in northern California's Trinity Alps in mid-August of 2008. Mark is an in-law of a canoeing buddy of mine, and he had come to Minnesota to paddle with us in the Boundary Waters Canoe Area Wilderness on two prior occasions. Both times Mark and Jen had invited me back to California for a back-packing trip, and the second time they extended the offer, I accepted.

The summer of 2008 was a heavy fire season, and evidence of light-ning-generated forest fires in the Trinity Alps was everywhere, as were the California Department of Forestry's efforts to maintain the blazes. Hotshot crews from Redding and Salmon River and several other places could not be missed. Mark's first two choices of routes for our trip were made off-limits by the fires, and our third choice required a substantial detour to even get to the trailhead. But hiking in the moun-tains was all new to me, and although Mark might have been disap-pointed by our inability to get to our first and second choices, it did not bother me at all.

The mid-afternoon of our third day on the trail found us walking down a path that would lead us to Mill Creek Lake, a lake that Mark had heard about and wanted to see firsthand. And it was there that we met a couple walking up the path toward us.

Mark is gregarious by nature, and he quickly engaged the couple in conversation, whereas my innate shyness prevented me from doing so. But I am a lawyer by training and profession, and even though my hearing has been dulled by too many years of way too loud music, I *am* a good and careful listener. And this is what I learned about the couple that we had just met:

They are from Oregon.

His name is Victor.

Her daughter is married to someone from Backus, Minnesota.

They are on their way to their favorite campsite.

They take sixty steps, then stop and count to ten, and repeat.

She didn't have a swimsuit and wanted us to respect their privacy when she went for a swim.

Victor is seventy-seven, and she is eighty-one.

And by the way, we missed the turn in the path that would take us to the lake that we were trying to get to.

Now realizing that we were headed in the wrong direction, we thanked them for the information, turned around and headed back up the trail. When we got to the crest of a hill we stopped and rested. We abandoned our goal of sleeping on the shore of elusive Mill Creek Lake, and instead Mark suggested that we camp at a certain spot across a different lake that was spread out before us. It appeared to be a nice site, but it also looked to me that *this* was where our newly-met acquaintances wanted to spend the night. I don't remember how we came to decide, but we ultimately moved on a bit. We ended up at an official campsite beyond the lake with lots of dirt but very little plant life to keep the dirt in place. As the day had worn on the wind did not abate, and Mark and I found ourselves camping in a dust bowl.

Dinner's conversation centered on the couple that we had met, the fact that they were a full generation older than either of us and that they were still hiking. Backpacking, no less! Both of them had been carrying full packs, including a tent, sleeping bags, sleeping pads, and everything else one needs to scratch out a home in the wilderness. Mark and I also addressed what, to me, was an important question crying out for an answer: whether or not the woman, whose name I unfortunately did not learn, would go swimming in the buff on this cool, windy, overcast late summer afternoon.

The Outdoors writer of the local newspaper in Duluth wrote a column many years ago, the gist of which was to never pass up the opportunity to go skinny-dipping. It is advice that I have taken to heart and that I try to follow whenever I can. I had hoped to go for a swim on this particular evening, but I was tired and hungry and just didn't feel up to it, so I took a pass.

Some time later, and after we had done our dishes and were just about ready to start the fire, who came ambling by but our two acquaintances, out for their evening walk. We exchanged pleasantries, talked about this and that, wished each other an enjoyable evening and bid each other good night. And as they were walking away from us I asked the eighty-one-year-old backpacker—a full twenty-four years older than me—if she had gone skinny-dipping.

"Yes," she replied.

I was not surprised, and the truth be told, I would have been a little bit disappointed if she had not.

The most acute information given to us by our newly met acquaintances on that day had been that we had missed the turn in the trail that would take us to our destination. This was information that was of immediate importance at the time, but which was of no use immediately afterwards. What *was* of significantly more importance was that these two elderly people, travelling at their own pace, were still doing what they obviously loved to do and that they were doing it together, in their own time, and on their own terms.

There is no doubt that our bodies wear out and disintegrate over time. The aging process is something that, as individuals, we cannot hope to conquer. The best we can do, when we go to bed at night, is to be in no worse shape when we awake in the morning. The best that we can do is to hold our own. For all of our spoken bravado, the simple fact is that our bodies *do* get tired, and after awhile, our bodies *do* betray us. But this is not to say that we should meekly lie down and let Nature commence its harvest. These two elderly backpackers had not lain down to await the inevitable. No one knows how much time they have left, but I have no doubt that they will use whatever time that remains.

And the next time I find myself declining to take advantage of the opportunity to swim in the buff because I am too tired or too cold or too busy, I will think back to my eighty-one-year-old backpacking friend, whose name I do not know, but whose spirit is akin to my own.

WHERE MEMORIES DREAM

MUSEUM VISITORS PLEASE TAKE NOTE: THIS RECENTLY DISCOVERED DIARY APPARENTLY DATES BACK TO THE EARLY 21ST CENTURY. IT WAS PRODUCED WELL BEFORE HUMANS REALIZED THAT INNUMERABLE SMALL, HOMOGENOUS PARTS OF THE EARTH, BY BEING REPEATEDLY VISITED BY HUMANS, HAD ACHIEVED THEIR OWN SPECIAL KIND OF CONSCIOUSNESS AS WELL AS THE ABILITY TO COMMUNICATE WITH OTHER SIMILAR "BEINGS." IT WAS ONLY RECENTLY THAT WE UNLOCKED THE SECRETS OF COMMUNICATION AMONG THESE INTELLIGENT LIFE FORMS THAT EXISTED AS PURE ENERGY. UNFORTUNATELY, A PORTION OF THE DIARY WAS DAMAGED DURING THE RETRIEVAL PROCESS, AND THE EXACT YEAR OF ITS KEEPING REMAINS UNKNOWN. THE AUTHOR, IF THAT IS WHAT WE ARE GOING TO CALL IT, WAS A CAMPSITE IN THE LEGENDARY BOUNDARY WATERS CANOE AREA WILDERNESS. THE CAMPSITE WAS LOCATED ON A SMALL ISLAND TOWARDS THE NORTHWESTERN SHORE OF A MEDIUM-SIZED LAKE. BUT WAS THE LAKE WEST OF ELY OR NORTHEAST OF ISABELLA? THE PHYSICAL CAMPSITE WAS DESTROYED DURING THE PERIOD KNOWN AS THE SECOND CONFLAGRATION, BUT WHAT BECAME OF ITS CONSCIOUSNESS? THERE IS STILL SO MUCH THAT WE DON'T KNOW.

PLEASE DO NOT TOUCH

FEBRUARY 7-10: How rare. And yet, how enjoyable! To be visited by campers in the dead of winter. I had the honor and privilege to host a group of three men and one woman during their four-day/three-night stay. The Forest Service rules prohibit winter campers from staying at established sites, the idea being to give us sites a chance to recover from the previous year's use. But the Forest Service really doesn't have to worry about winter campers. Winter campers tend to be more in tune with the environment and more aware of what is happening around themselves and to themselves. And they also are much more likely to respect me. I felt badly that I don't have any dead wood to offer them—the fair weather campers strip me clean every summer. But winter campers aren't lazy beings, and they aren't averse to travelling to get their wood. I think that my visitors had a good time. I felt lots of laughter coming from inside their tent. And like most other groups during any time of year, the mood of my campers changed as their stay lengthened. On the first night they were filled with joy and excitement. But the last night they were more subdued, most certainly because they realized that their trip, which they clearly enjoyed, was almost over. They all wished that they could come back earlier than they will be able to. They treated me with respect, and I will miss them.

MAY 12-14: Opening Day Weekend. I'm always guaranteed to have campers on Opening Day Weekend. This Opening Day Weekend it was forty-two degrees and misting. I'm home to four men who seemed to take their fishing seriously, given the fact that they were here in the first place. My rocks picked up another few scrapes of some man-made material called Kevlar and even some aluminum! I don't see as many Grumman or Alumicraft canoes as I used to, although either canoe, to me, is *the* classic Boundary Waters boat. I don't understand why campers go out of their way to go camping and then try and make it as much like home as they can when they are here. These campers weren't too bad as campers go, although they really should learn how to start and maintain a fire without tearing off fresh pieces of birch bark from my living trees. It's not healthy for my trees, and it doesn't look good either. But at least they did not saw off branches from live trees like those hooligans that I had to tolerate the year before. And they did a reasonably good job picking up after themselves. No bottles or cans, which is nice, but they did leave some nails in my birch tree that they tied their ropes to. I think that the Forest Service should teach campers how to tie knots. There are only two or three knots that a camper really needs to know and they are pretty easy to learn.

MAY 19-21: Two canoes paddled up, and one of the bowmen jumped out to size me up. They decided to pass on me and moved on, for reasons unstated.

MAY 26-29: This group of six amused me. Another drizzling weekend, and they stood around, hands in pockets, hoods up and over their heads, an occasional shiver running down their spines, all the while wishing that the weather would improve. They caught some fish and cleaned them on the rocks and left the remains on the shore. I wonder if the Forest Service will like that this year or not. It seems that the Forest Service goes back and forth on fish remains every few years: first you were to leave the remains on the rocks, then a few years later you had to throw them in the woods, and a few years after that you were told to leave them on shore. The same thing with garbage: first you were to burn it, and then a few years later you had to pack it out. This group did both. My fire grate is a mess. My campers packed out the cardboard and tried to burn the plastic. Not a pretty sight.

JUNE 2-4: School is out, or at least college is, because the drunks have finally arrived. This weekend I was abused by six young men in their early twenties who thought that the Boundary Waters is the place to come to drink, make a mess and make lots and lots of noise. Beer cans and glass pint bottles abound, and at least one glass bottle broke on the rock by the fire grate. They came with fishing rods (unused) and bait (died in the minnow bucket) and a loud CD player that disturbed the visitors that my sister site was hosting across the bay. I was desperately hoping for a visit from the Forest Service, but it was not to be. They left the following: dead beer cans, broken glass, tinfoil, plastic bags, twist ties, fishing lures, a pair of underwear, a knife, a roll of toilet paper, a puddle of bacon grease, a line wrapped around two of my trees (more campers that can't tie knots), six "D" batteries (five in the woods, laying where they landed after they were thrown, and one that rolled down into the water), paper bags and a magazine.

But I got the last laugh on one of them. He dropped the keys to his car, and I covered them up with some leaves that I had the wind blow over to my site. He had no idea that his keys were missing. I wished that I could be in the parking lot when he tried to unlock his car.

JUNE 6-8: This young married couple will be forever dear to me. They don't know it yet, but their firstborn-to-be was conceived under my birch trees. I hope that the three of them visit me next year—children are never too young to meet me. (This child will be female—I know these things.) I will respect their privacy and say nothing more about them. I wish them well.

JUNE 9-14: I'm not sure why two of these four people came at all. No skills, equipment that they didn't know how to use, constantly complaining about the weather (too wet, too cold, too windy). And to top it off, they were complaining that it's *my* fault, as if I had control over the rain, the temperature or the wind. But they saved their biggest complaints for the mosquitoes. Surely they must have been aware that mosquitoes abound in northern Minnesota lake country in the summer. I think that one couple convinced the other couple to try a canoe trip. I see a friendship breaking up.

JUNE 17: I had my latrine cleaned! I had my latrine cleaned!! I had my latrine cleaned!!!

JUNE 19-22: My clean latrine is now home to some uneaten food that my four campers elected to wrap in a plastic bag and throw away instead of packing out. I wonder what their kitchens look like at home. But they were lucky to get here in the first place. They were on the water with big winds that created big waves that none of them were ready for, and both canoes almost capsized. But Providence, or blind luck or some other not-yet-understood force, kept their canoes upright until they made it to my shore, where one of the campers promptly slipped on a rock and fell.

JUNE 24-26: Well, it's about time. My first dog of the camping season. Smiles is a rescue and has found a good home. Her humans treat her well, and she enjoyed herself. She left little reminders of herself all around me, but I didn't care. That's what dogs do. Smiles was mesmerized by one of my chipmunks, but as alert and quick as Smiles was, she could never catch the subject of her fascination. Dogs never treat me poorly, although humans frequently do. I wonder why that is. Humans are supposed to be smarter than their pets.

JUNE 27–JULY 1: I had an injury in camp. One of my campers slipped at the landing and fell on his wrist. He was in a fair amount of pain, and they decided to leave early. He felt badly that he had ruined the trip for his friends. Up to the point he fell, he and his three partners had made the most of me and my lake: up early in the morning to fish, day trips during the day, relaxing in hammocks in the late afternoon (these campers knew their knots!), interesting smells from the fire grate during their dinner hour, and some storytelling around a sensibly-sized campfire in the evening. I enjoyed their company.

JULY 2–5: This was the group that I've been waiting for: six friends on their annual Fourth of July camping trip. This is the sixth time (or is it the seventh?) trip that these three couples have made together, and this was the fourth time that they've stayed with me. I liked this group of campers. They were quiet and efficient, and they picked up after themselves well. "Leave no trace" certainly applied to these people. But what I really liked about them was their campfire discussions. Always wide-ranging, always thoughtful and always challenging. Their discussion on their second evening was particularly interesting to me, as they talked about how the Boundary Waters should be used. As best as I could tell, there were two "no motors" campers and two "yes motors" campers. The other two sat and listened—probably for the better. I've always thought that the "no motors" side of this argument tended to be somewhat arrogant in believing that the wilderness could only be enjoyed in a certain way (their way, which is "no motors allowed"), whereas the "yes motors" group tended to be somewhat selfish (we don't care how you use the wilderness, just let us use the wilderness the way we want to, without pausing to realize that, for some, the wilderness could only be enjoyed in the quiet solitude created by a lack of gasoline engines). I was bemused by it all. The land has been here forever, and it will be here forever, but humans in general, and individual humans in particular, will be here for only a very short period of time. The wilderness should be enjoyed, and if it's used with respect and if it is not abused, and if the people who use the wilderness are respectful of each other, I think that it can all work out.

JULY 6-9: The busy times are upon us. From now until late August it's going to be constant use of me and my sibling sites. This group paddled up to me, set up shop, stayed for two nights and left. They seemed to be in a hurry. Did they take the time to enjoy their visit? Did they notice the otter that had been watching them in the evenings?

JULY 9-13: I don't see many groups led by outfitters, I think because outfitters tend to travel the more "glamorous" routes, but this week I hosted a group of seven, consisting of one couple and their ten-year-old twins, a second couple, and their hired guide. The same group staying with me for a week can occasionally be tiring, but the presence of a guide makes it easier—guides don't do boneheaded things. They know where to pitch the tents, they know what wood will burn and they know their knots. One of the twins struggled during the week. I wished he would pay attention to where he was instead of missing his video games. The female half of the second couple was, I learned during the week, a well-known Hollywood-type that lived in southern California and came to Minnesota to canoe.

JULY 14-16: The drunks are back. Not the same group as I had to tolerate in early June, but to me, they are all the same. This group had a camper (about twenty-two) who liked to throw matches. How foolish! It's been pretty dry for several weeks. And his friend really should be more careful about diving off my rock face into the water. One of these days someone is going to get seriously hurt. More peeled birch bark. More noise, more garbage. But in the end, this group got what was coming to them, which was a routine visit by the Forest Service doing a permit check. This group had a permit, but it also had cans, which is a no-no. They were appropriately cited, and it'll cost them some money. The Forest Service confiscated their illegal cans, and the group, now without beer, decided to leave early. Good riddance!

JULY 19-23: My group of five had to do without campfires, as the Forest Service imposed a fire ban, but they made out all right. They enjoyed the loon serenade in the evenings and wished, as many, many campers do, that they could quit their day jobs and live out here. However, it's a wish that is not supported by a lot of thought. Living in the wilderness is a taxing and tiring affair, and most campers lack the endurance for the long haul. But they took a lot of pictures and some souvenirs, too (I won't miss an occasional pine cone or rock).

JULY 24-26:Another group of four "weekenders," getting out enjoying the woods when they can, although this group was on the sloppy side. When a camper sees some tinfoil in the fire grate, he or she is presented with a choice: Do they pack it out or do they leave it (after all, it's not their garbage, so why should they worry about it)? The sensible thing to do, disgusting as it is, is to clean up another's garbage and pack it out. The leader of this group had a different philosophy, however, which was: "There's already tinfoil in the fire grate, so I may as well throw my twisters in there as well. After all, better in the fire grate than out on the ground." Hard to believe but there really are people who think like that.

JULY 27-30:A group of four women, enjoying each other's company and enjoying the wilderness at the same time. A little weak on their knots, but they were quiet and aware that, in the evening, any noises they created will carry across the lake to my sibling sites, so they were careful to be quiet. They are four members of a group of seven, but only four could get out this summer. They do this every year. One of the four got up every morning and carried her mattress and sleeping bag to my exposed eastern rock face, snuggled into her sleeping bag (it was a bit chilly) and watched the sun rise. It's a special time of the day, and I'm surprised as to just how few of my campers make the effort to get up early. Different smells, different noises, different sights all await people who greet any day's sunrise.

JULY 31:A group of one! A solo canoeist, intent on paddling a route that he has thought of ever since he looked at his first Boundary Waters map so many years ago. A solo canoe, one large pack, a small day pack, an extra paddle and a compass. He's having a grand time, travelling on his own schedule, going where he wants to go when he wants to go there. I was happy to have him with me tonight. I rest well when I'm visited by campers who appreciate me. He left early in the morning, paddling to the west. He was here for only a short while, but I am sad to see him leave. The lake was calm as he paddled off, and his ever widening wake lasted a long time. Tonight he'll be sleeping at one of my sibling sites three lakes west of me. I know that that site will enjoy his attention.

AUGUST 1-4: I hosted my first wedding! Weddings in the Boundary Waters are not uncommon—my sibling site three lakes to the east has hosted three in seven years—but this was my first. The bride and groom, the best man, the maid of honor, the officiant and her spouse and four other close friends rounded out the wedding party. They were over the nine-person limit by one, but under these circumstances, would the Forest Service have objected? They were a well-behaved group. Sixty-six degrees with a noisy wind but mostly sunny skies. When they left there was still rice around the campsite, thrown by the well-wishers, but I didn't mind. "The bride wore Gore-tex" seemed to be an amusing tagline throughout their stay.

AUGUST 5-9: I note with sadness the passing of my big bull snapping turtle. As with all things that live, it was his time to die, and die he did, about seventy-five feet up from the water's edge and under a large, spreading fern. His death, and his presence before his death, went unnoticed by the group of four campers that were staying with me. For all of the many things that campers notice when they stay with me, the vast majority of happenings that take place all around them go unnoticed. This is not a criticism of my campers, just an observation. Watching a loon teach its chick how to feed is a fascinating thing for city folk to observe, but really no more fascinating than watching two spiders, one the parent to the other, in a wresting match that can only end in death for one of them. My snapping turtle will provide food for many creatures, both his size and smaller, millions of them microscopic in size. His shell will ultimately dissolve, and it, along with his other parts, will provide nutrition for my soil and, ultimately, food for my plants. Such is the way of living things. The land is immortal, but living things are not. My campers left tired but relaxed, unaware of most of the many dramas that had taken place all around them.

AUGUST 11–13: Two people who left the city to "get away from it all" and brought it all with them. Laptop computers really don't hurt anything, I suppose, but do they really belong here? One of my campers thought so. I'm not sure if he was doing work or not. I don't want to find out either. His partner was the better camper of the two. They did no harm, they broke no laws and they hurt no one. But I'm not really sure why they bothered to come in the first place. In any event, they did no damage, and they told each other that they had a good time. But they neglected to watch the Perseid meteor shower. To each his own, I guess.

AUGUST 15: Another solo camper, this one going in the opposite direction from the solo camper two weeks ago. Competent and efficient, with an eye on what's really important, which pretty much describes most solo campers. The beauty of solo camping, I have observed, is that one does what one wants to do when one wants to do it. And of course, nothing gets done unless the solo camper does it. This camper brought along her black lab for company. I sensed from the dog that his human's name was Jill. Animals have their own intelligence and humans are arrogant in believing that they don't. I'm not sure which of the two enjoyed their stay with me more. When she left, the black lab sat proudly in the bow, snapping at the hard-to-see but very numerous insects.

AUGUST 16–20: Every year I am visited by numerous "gear freaks" as they are called by their condescending trip mates. If it's new, they have it, be it a stove, a water bottle, a water filter, a sleeping bag, a tent, a canoe, a paddle, an oven, or anything else that the manufacturer has marketed by claiming it to be "new and improved." No harm done, I suppose, but I wonder, "Why?" One of my campers had a new stove that works, I'm sure, exactly as well as the one he left at home. Another of my campers caught a four-pound walleye, left it on the stringer, and when he returned several hours later, found the remnants of his future dinner, it having already become the dinner for one of my resident raccoons. He won't make this mistake a second time. But that's how many of my campers learn. That night a gust of wind brought down a dead branch from one of my birch trees, and it landed perilously close to their tent. They didn't think to check above them when they rigged their tent, but they'll check overhead the next time they are making camp.

AUGUST 20-23: No guests. I wonder why. The weather is certainly nice enough. My sibling sites reported decreased attendance as well. I wonder if the professional football season has started yet. I take the time to recover. While doing so an otter brought me news of one of my sibling sites on the lake to the east. The Forest Service is taking out the site. Years of use and overuse had taken its toll. The site will be relocated three hundred yards to the south. The fire grate will be taken out, the sitting logs will be moved around and the box latrine will be pulled. In a few short years the site will look like it had never been there at all. All that will remain will be a red dot on an old map. But what happens to the memories? Do the memories get relocated, too? That's a question for my Fourth of July philosopher campers. I look around me. I'm still in good shape. But that broken glass left by that camper two months ago is starting to loom larger and larger. The branch missing from my birch tree was surely noticed by the Forest Service when it was here to clean my latrine. My birch trees are healthy, but lazy campers without basic fire building skills tear off the bark from my trees. Will the Forest Service at some point decide that I need to be relocated? What will happen to *my* memories?

AUGUST 24-27: Three fathers and three daughters, the dads in their forties and the girls almost, but not quite, young women. This group has been to this area before, and I think that I saw them from afar two years ago. These six have done a father/daughter trip every year for the last ten years, but this might be their last trip. And if they do come again, it won't be for a long time. Boyfriends and soccer and other distractions are already on the near horizon, and future trips are probably a long way off. The fathers understood that this might be their last trip with their daughters and were relishing these moments with their kin. The daughters understood that this might be their last trip with their fathers but did not understand the significance of it, nor could they. What they had in youth they lacked in wisdom. One father remembered a skinned knee on his then five-year-old daughter from years ago. The daughter fondly remembered being hugged by her father at the time and asked her dad about it. But her dad could not answer and had to walk away. He shed a tear that got lost in the dew. Three nights of campfires produced little discussion but many memories. The fathers wondered where the time had gone. Their daughters didn't yet understand time. It was a bittersweet trip for the dads. They paddled out on the last day, the dads taking their time, trying to make the trip last just a little longer, remembering past trips. The daughters pulled on their paddles trying to go faster—they were already thinking about who they were going to call when they got home. The afternoon's temperature was a little cooler than it had been. A gust of wind sent a little chill through the fathers. Their daughters did not notice.

AUGUST 27–SEPTEMBER 5: The Rangers are coming. It's that time of year for Boy Rangers to climb into cars and vans in Illinois and come up for their annual canoe trip. I saw six groups of three canoes each—thirty-six people total, one adult for every five Rangers. Lots of testosterone coming my way, and I felt I was sure to end up with a group of nine. And I did. Rangers are good campers, and their chaperones watched them closely. They stayed for a week, and when they left there was a lot of marshmallow remains on the rocks around the fire grate. But that evening's rain washed it off easily. The Rangers caught lots of fish, and by the end of the week some of them had learned how to clean a fish efficiently. One of the Rangers caught a fishhook very close to his eye, but all good Rangers are prepared, and it was removed without a problem. The adults tried their turns telling stories, but the Rangers were better fish cleaners than the adults were storytellers. Many of these Rangers had been to the Boundary Waters before, and although no one knew it yet (except me), the seven Rangers that I had at my site included two future Outward Bound guides and an emergency wilderness first responder. Notions of excitement and adventure, if planted young, can grow to be fulfilling careers. The Rangers took advantage of their time here.

SEPTEMBER 8–10: Your basic three-day/two-night trip for two people. Ben and Joanie had no trouble getting a permit—the rush is over.

And I can start to rejuvenate myself. Still, I enjoy my campers. Good feelings and warm memories keep the land young, and these two, both in their early twenties, already respect the wilderness.

While they are out and about on the lake I took stock of the things that happened to me during the year. Many visitors came to stay with me, and for the most part, they were respectful. Some clunkers pounded nails where knots would have worked better. Others left garbage that people they never met had to clean up. Bits of broken glass will litter me for thousands of years. There's a beer can that sank eighteen feet from shore. It's in water twelve feet deep. No one knows it's there but me. It doesn't belong there, but there's nothing that I can do about it. A few minor injuries, but nothing that'll interfere with anyone's life in the future. A baby was conceived under my birch trees. And a wedding took place at the fire grate. Either event more than makes up for the beer can. Many good times but also some disappointments. Frustrations about the weather, the poor fishing, the prohibition against building a fire. Continued attempts to make my landing a little easier to step onto from a canoe. And like all such previous attempts, this year's efforts are met with limited success. To be honest, I like the landing just the way it is. Some new cuss words about the mosquitoes that I'll have to share with my sibling campsites. They will be amused, and I look forward to hearing about their visitors. Some good stories around the campfires. Some sadness, even some anger, and some hurt feelings, but lots of camaraderie—*lots* of camaraderie—and much friendship and much love. Humans with completely different experiences and outlooks on life fondly enjoying each other's company. Warm feelings among friends who don't see each other as much as they'd like to. Lots of laughter. Smiling faces. Lots of skinny-dipping. Lots of barking dogs and some crying babies, and a few crying adults as well. Many promises to return, promises all well-intentioned when made, but many of which are destined to be abandoned after the thrill of wilderness camping has faded. But many of the promises are destined to be kept. Imagine: New Year's resolutions made in September! Regrets of youth misspent, but appreciation for the time still left. Anticipation of the time not yet used, the life yet to be. Planning for next year's trips. Someone's goal to canoe, pull or stumble down the Frost River. One of these times he'll make it. (I know these things.)

I so enjoy humans!

All of the people who stay with me mature in their own time. The person who cut the branch from one of my birch trees last year might grow up to remember what he did with shame. Or he might not give it a second thought. All in all, people must have a good time, because many of the same people keep coming back, and oftentimes they bring with them people who have never been here before. I know that I'll see some of them for many years. There are others that I know I'll never see again. But every year there are new people who have never been to the wilderness before. *Every year!*

I am hopeful. And when an immortal spirit is hopeful, there's hope for mankind.

OCTOBER 13-15: The leaves were past their peak, but there were still colors galore as four people paddled up to me on their annual "shoulder season trip," taking advantage of the colorful leaves and the blue sky and noting the chill in the air and the cold on the small of their backs when they stood to walk away from the campfire. Most of the birds that were going to move on had already done so, although a few Juncos were picking at some rice kernels that they had discovered, left over from the wedding. On a dare, one of the campers went for a swim and wished he hadn't. One of the women sat on the rocks, took in the early evening stillness and reflected on her year and what she wanted to do in the future. They packed up and left, making sure to put out their campfire before they did so. It was a last, little touch that I appreciated. It showed that they respected me.

It is time for me to rest. As much as I enjoy my campers, I need this time alone. I also need to mingle with my sibling spirits from the other campsites. My trees and bushes and grasses are already dormant. I know that I'll be visited by moose and Canada Jays and otters and chickadees in the coming months. I'm gratified to know that I provide recreation and rest and sustenance and solace for many diverse and disparate beings, and it's that feeling of fulfillment that keeps my spirit young.

But now I must sleep.

BIBLIOGRAPHY

"WHADDYA MEAN I CAN'T HAVE A MOTOR ON THIS LAKE?" (Page 115)

Boundary Waters Canoe Area (Robert Beyer) Wilderness Press 1979

Boundary Waters Canoe Area: A Contentious History (Leif Enger) Minnesota Public Radio: July 17, 1998

Glacial Geology of the Boundary Waters Canoe Area Wilderness (Rachel M. Bursheim, Leah M. Gruhn, Jere A. Mohr)

GORP – Boundary Waters – Natural History: Geology

Paddler's Guide to the Boundary Waters Canoe Area (Michael Duncanson) W.A. Fisher Company 1976

ABOUT THE AUTHOR

Steve Coz (as in Cozy) has done over 60 camping trips in the Boundary Waters Canoe Area Wilderness, of which half were in a canoe and half were in the winter. He likes the contrasts between winter and summer camping/trekking. While doing these trips he has traveled extensively along the Minnesota/Ontario border. In addition, he has done a dozen overnight backpacking trips on the Superior Hiking Trail and another dozen winter or summer canoe or camping trips in other locations. His winter and summer camping trips have taken him to Minnesota's BWCAW, the subarctic of Manitoba, Nunavut (part of the old Northwest Territories), Ontario, Quebec, Labrador, Maine, Wisconsin, California, Montana and Wyoming. He has visited all 66 of Minnesota's state parks.

He is a Superior Hiking Trail (SHT) section leader, and for the last 18 years has been responsible for maintaining a section of the SHT. In addition to assisting in SHT trail construction and leading organized SHT hikes, he is an avid skier, bicyclist, hiker, amateur astronomer, birder and practitioner of ashtanga and vinyasa flow yoga.

Coz is a spouse and parent. He retired from practicing law with an emphasis on criminal defense as a public defender, after 33 years.

Coz says, "My scariest wilderness moment was in a solo canoe on Cherokee Lake in early June 2009 in rough water and big winds while separated from other people on the trip—my canoe was shaking and I couldn't get it to stop." "My most enduring wilderness frustration: I have not yet traveled a 3-mile gap between the end of the Isabella River and the middle of Bald Eagle Lake in the BWCA—maybe next year."

The proudest moment of his life was holding his 15-month-old son while taking an oath on his son's behalf at his naturalization ceremony that made his son a citizen of the United States in May of 1990.

Other Savage Press Books

REGIONAL HISTORY, MEMOIR

A Life in Two Worlds by Betty Powell Skoog with Justine Kerfoot
Beyond the Freeway by Peter J. Benzoni
Crocodile Tears and Lipstick Smears by Fran Gabino
DakotaLand by Howard Jones
Fair Game by Fran Gabino
Journey into Joy by Jill Downs
Memories of Iron River by Bev Thivierge
Stop in the Name of the Law by Alex O'Kash
Superior Catholics by Cheney and Meronek
Widow of the Waves by Bev Jamison

BUSINESS

Dare to Kiss the Frog by vanHauen, Kastberg & Soden
SoundBites, a Business Guide for Working With the Media
  by Kathy Kerchner

POETRY

A Woman for All Time by Evelyn Gathman Haines
Eraser's Edge by Phil Sneve
Gleanings from the Hillside by E.M. Johnson
In The Heart of the Forest by Diana Randolph
I Was Night by Bekah Bevins
Papa's Poems by Nick Glumac
Pathways by Mary B. Wadzinski
Philosophical Poems by E.M. Johnson
Poems of Faith and Inspiration by E.M. Johnson
Portrait of the Mississippi by Howard Jones
The Morning After the Night She Fell Into the Gorge by Heidi Howes
Thicker Than Water by Hazel Sangster
Treasures from the Beginning of the World by Jeff Lewis

HUMOR

Baloney on Wry by Frank Larson
Jackpine Savages by Frank Larson

OTHER BOOKS AVAILABLE FROM SP

Blueberry Summers by Lawrence Berube
Dakota Brave by Howard Jones
Spindrift Anthology by The Tarpon Springs Writers Group

To order additional copies of

Where Memories Dream

Call:

1-800-732-3867

or Email:

mail@savpress.com

You may purchase copies online at:

www.savpress.com

where

Visa/MC/Discover/American Express/Echeck

are accepted via PayPal